‘

While Manasij gave me a premium economy status, I would any day spend time in the last row of the economy class with him if these are the stories I will get to hear. Enthralling, real, brutally honest – *The Economy Class Founder* took me on a journey that felt like mine.

ANKUR WARIKOO

’

The Economy Class Founder

Manasij Ganguli

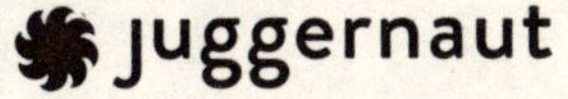

JUGGERNAUT BOOKS
C-I-128, First Floor, Sangam Vihar, Near Holi Chowk,
New Delhi 110080, India

First published by Juggernaut Books 2023

10 9 8 7 6 5 4 3 2 1

P-ISBN: 9788195996971
E-ISBN: 9789353451639

Typeset in Adobe Caslon Pro by R. Ajith Kumar, Noida

Printed at Thomson Press India Ltd

To all the unknown and unnamed dreamers who dared and built something – for daring needs to be celebrated.

The fallen must have arisen.

Connect with the Author

Contents

Preface

Amazon, Google, Facebook, Airbnb, Paytm, WhatsApp, Zomato, Tesla, Uber, Flipkart, Ola, Jeff Bezos, Steve Jobs, Mark Zuckerberg, Elon Musk, unicorns, venture capitalists, Silicon Valley...

In today's world, these names feel almost mythical and larger than life. Pop culture has elevated these founders into superhumans, almost like Marvel's X-Men – wrapped in indestructible shields of awesomeness and coolness, much like the billionaire-philanthropist-playboy-genius Tony Stark, aka Ironman.

But beneath the glitz and glam are the real stories. You don't get to hear the real stories. They don't go like Bruce Wayne building his Batmobile in his multimillion-dollar mansion with his billions.

Real stories are brutal. A real story is being rejected by 119 investors – yes, that's my rejection count. I still have all of the 119 on my WhatsApp and LinkedIn as connections. A real story is being rejected by 500+ customers – yes, that's the number of people who saw our innovation but didn't believe us anyway.

A real story is not about the high of creativity, it's the mind-numbing fear of going bankrupt, not once, not twice, but three times. The first time, we had only 28 days to survive until we got our first customer cheque. The second time, we had 42 days when we got the next round of investment. The third time, we had six days of money left when we sold the start-up for ₹100 crore! Now, if your eyes popped at ₹100 crore, let me tell you, it is just chump change in the world of start-ups.

Artist's impression of yours truly
A more handsome Manasij Ganguli…

There is a caste system among founders fuelled by how much money they have made. The top tier is held by founders like Jeff Bezos and Elon Musk, who have their private space vehicles – let's call them space class founders. Close on their heels are the mega-billionaires like Mark Zuckerberg, Bill Gates and his ilk – the private jet founders.

Then you have founders with a few billion like Girish of Freshworks and the Bansals of Flipkart – the first class founders. Folks who have a couple of hundred million assets like Kunal Shah of Cred and Byju Ravindran of BYJU's are business class founders. Ankur Warikoo of Nearbuy and Karan Bajaj of WhiteHat Jr are premium economy founders.

I am the founder on the middle seat of the last row of the plane who jumps each time the toilet flushes – I am an economy class founder. That's the value of a ₹100 crore exit. In the start-up world, I am a nobody.

This is my story. This is a true story. All the characters in this story are real people – I have changed some of their names to protect their privacy.

I am no hero. The characters in my story are no heroes either. But together we built and scaled a unique business.

In 2019, when we sold our business, our software was planning 1.5 billion garments each year – i.e., 2 per cent of what the world wears annually! That is a huge global market share for a start-up. We were doing business in 16 countries, and our business took us to 40 countries in five years. We were the first tech start-up to raise venture capital (VC) money and make an exit in the Apparel Tech sector. We opened a sector that didn't exist before. The person who is at the frontline in an assault takes the most amount of fire, and so did we. So, there is no dearth of passion, drama, action and emotion in the story.

Who should read this book?

If you are interested in start-ups, this book is for you. If you are planning to create your own start-up, this book is for you. I have put together my personal experience of building an international business on a shoestring budget and if my story helps you, I will consider it worthwhile. If you are star-struck by the start-up world, you should read this book for a hard reality check. If you think creating a start-up is easy, read this book. You might change your opinion.

If you plan to work for a start-up, this book is for you – it's not easy to work for start-ups and this book will give you a glimpse of that. If your friends and family work for start-ups, this book is for you – you might get a sense of what their lives are like and how much of a challenge it is to work in a fast-paced, chaotic world.

If you are a venture capitalist or an angel investor, this book is for you – next time a dreamy founder meets you, you might treat them a little better. If you think building a start-up is a shortcut to getting rich, this book is for you – you should, especially, read the last few chapters! If you think the start-up world is free from the glass ceilings of race, gender, income inequality, etc., – this book will dispel those doubts for you.

When I sit back and recount my journey, it looks unreal to me. We, the four founders, had no money; we did not know any investors; we did not know our customers; we had a team that was fresh out of college (average age was 23); and we started a business in a sector that had seen no historical success in tech and had no investors backing it. Yet, we managed to create a decent-sized international business. It had all been incredibly improbable.

But then, improbable stories make for the best stories. So are you ready?

Let's go do this . . .

Part I

Let's Go Do This . . .

The start . . .

The rejections . . .

The first investor . . .

The first customer . . .

The first employees . . .

The hardest choice . . .

1

Live Today, Fight Another Day

It was 4 a.m.

The long corridors of the Ninoy Aquino International Airport in Manila were mostly empty. There were very few fliers for the early morning flight to Singapore.

I was still reeling from my four-hour-long car ride from Angeles, some 100 kilometres from Manila. I had pulled off a 24-hour work trip that involved two international flights, eight hours of driving and another eight of hectic negotiations with customers in two countries. I had had almost no sleep in the last 24 hours and was looking forward to getting some shut-eye on the flight.

The work wasn't done yet. I had a full day of running around in Singapore before I could take the evening flight back to New Delhi. I had to meet an Indo-Chinese VC fund for a discussion on the next round of investment, conduct an important interview for a senior sales profile for Vietnam and take a customer meeting for an Indonesian group that had stubbornly refused to complete a $100,000 deal unless they met the CEO of the start-up whose tech they were considering buying. That would be me! I looked at the phone and it showed some dozen unread emails . . .

That didn't cheer me up.

With 30 minutes to board, I made a quick dash to the

washroom. That year, the Manila airport had been voted the worst by Tripadvisor's international travellers' community. I went into the last washroom at the end of the corridor. It was not well-lit and the floor was full of water. I, too, was tempted to cast another downvote on Tripadvisor.

When I came out of the toilet cubicle, I saw a big guy standing to the right of the stall door. Without warning, he landed a mighty punch in my rib cage. I fell to the ground, seeing stars. Before I could take a breath, someone was putting a big plastic bag on my face. Now my head was inside a plastic bag and I was face-first, lying in the water on the cold floor. I was grunting and trying to breathe. The air had been squeezed out of me.

That's when I realized there were three men. One guy had bagged my head and was squatting over me with his knee knifing my back. Another was holding my legs firmly pinned to the ground. The third one, possibly the guy who had punched me, had twisted my arms and was pinning them to my back.

The men started to search me.

'Wallet?'

'Dollars?'

The guy who had my arms pinned barked into my ears. I tried to say something but couldn't speak clearly due to shock and breathlessness.

They roughly sat me up against the wall. One of them pulled the plastic bag up to my nose and mouth, keeping my eyes fully covered. I took the deepest breath of my life.

They searched my jacket and could not find anything except my passport and mobile.

'You no money?'

'No dollars?'

The guy barked again and landed an iron-handed slap on my cheek. My left cheek and jaw went numb and began to burn.

I told them I kept my wallet in my laptop bag. The barking guy hissed into my ears, 'No noise. I will kill you.' I felt a metallic prick against my throat.

They found money in my wallet. I had US Dollars, Singapore Dollars, Pounds, Euros and Hong Kong Dollars – thanks to my crazy travel schedules. They took it all – it was about $300 or ₹25,000.

The atmosphere relaxed a bit.

They have got what they wanted, I thought, *now they will let me go*.

But something was wrong. The same guy asked me, 'You go Singapore?'

'Yes,' I said.

'No Bangkok?'

'No,' I said.

They started to argue among themselves. It looked like they had taken me for a passenger going to board the Bangkok-bound flight just about to depart. Now they had a problem. I had 30 minutes before boarding and that's a lot of time to make trouble. The first guy kept the edge of the knife (I don't know if it was a knife) firmly at my throat. By this time, the initial shock of the attack was over.

The three men were agitated. The guy who was talking to me all the while – clearly the leader of the pack – again reiterated his threat. Now, I heard a fourth guy's voice.

'No noise. Or I kill you.' The leader guy repeated his threat.

Suddenly, they all fell silent. The silence was chilling. I couldn't see anything.

What were these guys up to?

Were they going to slash my throat?

They had made a mistake.

Had they panicked?

The suspense was tearing me apart. I tried to speak, and the leader guy landed another slap on my face. We all fell silent. Somewhere a tap was dripping. It felt like an eternity.

I heard the announcement of my flight boarding. I wanted to tell them but was too afraid. The leader was getting more and more agitated, and I was getting equally worried. Then, I heard my name being announced. I tried to gesture to them. The guys had my passport. They also heard the name in the announcement, and I heard them try to say my name.

Finally, the leader stood me up. He gave my laptop bag to me and said, 'You go flight. No turn back.'

I heard the main door of the washroom open. The bright light dazzled me. The plastic bag was off my head.

I heard my name again on the announcement.

'Passenger Mr Ganguli, this is the last and final call . . .'

I began to run. I was free!

I reached the boarding area. The flight crew was gesturing me to hurry up. I stopped.

What do I do? I pondered, *Shall I go and complain to the authorities?*

'Sir, do you want to board the flight?'

The flight attendant was visibly pissed at me for baulking at the last step. If only she knew.

Should I file a complaint to the authorities? But I haven't seen their faces. Also, I will miss the flight. And the meetings in Singapore? And the flight to New Delhi . . . it would cost a lot.

'Sir, do you want to go? Yes or no?' Another threat.

'Yes.'

I walked into the plane and sank into my seat. The flight was mostly empty; luckily, I had no co-passenger sitting beside me. My face was burning from the blows. My clothes were wet and smelly. My hands and feet were shaking and my vision was blurred. I took out the air sickness bag and started blowing into it with force – grunting and panting. I was having a full-blown panic attack.

I had three important engagements in Singapore. I needed to convince a prospective investor, a prospective customer and a prospective employee that we were a great start-up with good technology and an awesome team. And that I was a great dynamic guy who they should trust. And no matter how hard the situation is, we would never give up. But here I was hyperventilating into an air-sickness bag!

By the time the plane reached cruising altitude, I had calmed down. I was seeing colour again. I had made peace with the fact that I had not gone after these guys.

Our small start-up would have lost a lot of money for all the flights that I would have missed.

Not to mention that my meetings with the customers and investors would have to be cancelled. It is hard to find an Indo-Chinese investor like the one who had agreed to see me in Singapore. There was a $100,000 deal to be completed – not a small deal!

And it's hard to find good employees. So, in every way, I had taken the right decision.

Live today, fight another day, I told myself.

Little did I know that, eventually, the investor would not invest, the customer would not buy and the employee would not join!

How ironic was that?

Meet the co-founders – let's unleash
Abhishek, Mausmi and Bratish…

2

How Ironic Was That?

If I were to pick a date, place and event that was the genesis of our start-up story, we would need to dial back our clocks to 19 August 1996, to a rainy Monday in Patna. My first day at college.

I had just completed my Class 10 board exams and had enrolled in Patna's Science College. It was the city's most sought-after college for classes 11 and 12. That day I met Mausmi. We were both 16. She was a beautiful young girl who had a spark in her big dark brown-eyes and an unusual calmness in her voice. I was smitten by her charm and poise. I knew immediately I wanted her to be my girlfriend. Who knew that the girl I would meet as a teenager and fall in love with would one day become my life partner and eventually co-founder of our start-up!

In 1996, Patna was a seriously small-town kind of place. Every kid growing up in the city had one ambition – to leave it. My father was a professor of chemistry at Science College. My mother was a homemaker and lorded over the ten thousand books we had in our house. So I grew up in an academically hospitable climate. As a result, I also knew that I was supposed to study hard, get an engineering degree and get out of Patna.

Apart from having no real economic future, Patna was a chaotic city hamstrung with dirt and grime, with poverty and corruption.

Young people had few opportunities to meet, court and fall in love as it was a really puritan society, and vigilante moral policing was rampant. If you wanted to date a girl, you had to be prepared for nasty surprises. I was also about to find out the price I had to pay for being with Mausmi.

It didn't help that she was the most popular girl in class. She was very warm, approachable and had an air of amicability about her. We became friends very quickly and would spend a lot of time together chatting – which upset a lot of people. After class, I would walk her to her chemistry tuition class and, usually, one of her stalkers would follow us. She would be super calm about being stalked while it always creeped me out. One evening, one of her stalkers walked up to me and showed me a poem he had written for her. He warned me to stay away from her or face some serious consequences. I ignored the guy.

Then a deluge of harassment fell upon me. I started receiving letters at home, filled with abuse and threats. My parents didn't think the letters were a big deal, which was a relief.

But that wasn't the end of it. There were threatening phone calls, and on the college campus, I received threats from some seniors as well. Everyone had one piece of advice for me – stick to your studies and leave Mausmi alone.

She received calls too, where guys would ask her to dump me and cite all my so-called flaws. She dealt with them calmly as she knew any disgruntled reaction would make things worse for me. I think I was never physically harmed because of how expertly she handled these guys.

The vilest attack came on a cool Monday morning in early November. As I rode into campus on my cycle, I saw my friends standing with ashen faces. The walls were graffitied with the choicest abuses against me. Everyone saw it – all my friends, all the students, all my teachers, my father, everyone. My friends and I spent the day scrubbing the walls of the filth.

Initially, the harassment would trouble me. It soon became a part of my daily routine and I started ignoring them. Every time anyone said I couldn't be seen with Mausmi, it only strengthened my resolve. She was very supportive, and through the madness, we got closer and closer.

I endured the harassment for two years and finally left Patna for Ranchi, where I got into the Birla Institute of Technology (BIT), Mesra, for an undergraduate degree in Electrical and Electronics Engineering. Around 300,000 students had appeared for the engineering entrance examination across India for only 300 seats and I got through with a rank of 42.

Mausmi, in the meantime, moved to Noida for her engineering degree. Despite being 1,500 kilometres apart, we kept in touch. There was no widely available internet in 1998, nor was there any mobile network. Phone calls were limited to STD (State Trunk Dialing) and cost as much as ₹24 per minute. So, we wrote each other long letters and spoke once a week for two–three minutes in the dead of the night when the call rates would be a fourth of the peak rates.

We would get to meet in Patna during our college breaks. It was a relief to meet her without the harassers of the past. Most of them, whom I know by name, are now working in large multinational companies and are vocal on social media on equality and freedom and gender justice, and are avid nationalists.

In Ranchi, I discovered my second love – computers, more so, algorithms. I had got into programming as a teenager, playing around with Basic, but the engineering stint injected steroids to this interest, and I had fun times programming with my year 2000 model, state-of-the-art, Pentium One processor of 233 MHz, 32

MB RAM with an unbelievable 10 GB hard disk that seemed it could store the world in it!

By 2000, four years into our relationship, Mausmi and I were exchanging emails and instant messages on Yahoo Messenger over very patchy dial-up connections. But we never stopped writing letters to each other. Today, we have over 200 letters and cards, neatly arranged in a cardboard box, that we wrote to each other for over six years.

In June 2002, I began my work life at TCS, the biggest software services firm in India. The work was interesting initially and then gradually the service industry started to bore me. The only good thing in my life was Mausmi. I had moved to Noida, and we were living together. It was not something we would talk about in the open, and it was considered quite scandalous in those days to live together without being married.

It also had an obvious downside – we could not get good homes on rent. The only solution to living in peace, in a decent house, was to get married. And so, after eight years of dating and living together, we finally got married on 14 December 2004. We were 24.

Mausmi completed her engineering degree and enrolled in a postgraduate course at NIFT, India's premier fashion institute, by securing a rank of 14 in the national entrance exam. It was at NIFT that Mausmi would get exposed to the trillion-dollar-sized apparel and fashion business and find solutions to some of the long-standing unsolved issues on which we would one day build our start-up.

In the meantime, I decided to join a very interesting small company (around 500 people) in Noida named Impetus Technologies. Impetus was doing product development for US-based clients, and I joined their R&D team as a technical lead.

In 2006, cloud computing was slowly and steadily becoming a

game-changing technology. We were discussing how to create a practice group in Impetus to create cloud technologies. Mausmi and I had gone on a short vacation to Ladakh – my favourite place on the planet – and when I returned, I was told that someone at Impetus had created a private cloud.

I was intrigued. I knew no one in Impetus who could do this and that too in so few days.

I logged in sceptically, but after a couple of hours of use, I was very impressed with the work. It was indeed a proper, working private cloud!

Apparently, Impetus had hired a new guy and he had built this in his free time when he was awaiting the allocation of a project. I wanted to meet this wizard. That afternoon, I met a guy wearing an oversized tee and worn-out denim with flip-flops. His eyes were red and swollen, he wore a three-day beard and spoke in a funny, accented English, which screamed Hindi-medium schooling in North India – so much for a wizard! I am a bit ashamed to admit that I was taken in by this initial impression and wasn't too impressed by this guy.

But I changed my mind as soon as we began to talk. He explained with absolute clarity how he had built the private cloud. It was amazing. Later I found out that he looked so dishevelled because his wife had been admitted to a hospital with a very complicated pregnancy, and he was juggling a new job and a personal emergency. What struck me was how he hadn't allowed this to affect him and managed to deliver a terrific piece of work. That was my first meeting with Abhishek Srivastava.

Abhishek and I would become very good friends and work on many challenging projects together and one day build our start-up as co-founders.

By 2007, the wind of the financial crisis was blowing hard. Companies around the world were feeling the heat of the meltdown of subprime mortgages in the US. Layoffs were common, and Impetus was no exception. It decided to lay off the non-critical resources, which were mainly the fresh graduates. They were divided into groups and given a free hand to innovate and showcase their work in a competition for the best innovation award in the R&D division. If their product didn't cut ice, they could be let go. Thankfully, I was not given the job to make that decision.

I did end up checking out one of the group's demos. They had built a fully functional online whiteboard-sharing application over the browser. I thought it was unbelievably ahead of its time (there was no large-scale online whiteboard-sharing application in 2007). The young engineers had named their product Virtua-Pedagogy, a marketing disaster, but it was high-quality tech and I pitched strongly for the group.

Because of my backing, the Virtua-Pedagogy team demonstrated their innovation in a shootout for the best innovation award of the R&D division. In a way, I was also on trial for sticking my neck out for these young engineers. Abhishek and I had also our R&D product to showcase – by that time we were well-known tech experts in Impetus. That evening, Abhishek and my project came runners-up. The product that won was called Virtua-Pedagogy!

The leader of this talented pack was a solidly built, slightly plump, round-faced, quiet chap named Bratish Goswami. His poise and gravity was immense, and he was exceptionally mature for a fresh engineering graduate. That was my first brush with Bratish. We became friends and executed many challenging projects together.

As destiny would have it, Bratish would become one of the four co-founders of our start-up.

Abhishek, Bratish, Mausmi and I would take off on long weekend drives near Delhi.

Abhishek's wife, Mitali, a fantastic cook and a great homemaker, would supply us with sumptuous meals while we would sit around and discuss life and times.

At the end of each of these outings, Abhishek would always introduce his three-pronged agenda to all conversations. First, he would pester us to check out the next happening restaurant in town. Second, he would push us to plan the next weekend getaway to some exotic resort. And finally, he would tell us we had to start-up.

I didn't know where Abhishek got the courage to dream about a start-up. Mausmi and I had almost no savings. This meant having a paycheck was important. Abhishek had a similar background. He had lost his dad at an early age and had been working from a very young age to support his family and pay for his education. Now he had a kid and a wife who were dependent on him. Bratish came from an even more humble background. It was only after Bratish got his job that his family saw a colour television and a washing machine for the first time! His father needed dialysis twice a week. Bratish was the only earning member in his family of four. He had no savings either.

Our cumulative bank balance was less than ₹5 lakh ($8,000). None of us had any family money to fall back on. Yet, at some point, we all quit our jobs and plunged into the risky start-up life.

Who in their right mind would do this?

3

Who in Their Right Mind Would Do This?

The snow was almost one foot deep. There was no way I could continue to cycle any more.

So, I got down from my mountain bike and started wading through the ice and slush. The road ahead had a serpentine queue of vehicles stuck in the snow looking like dead carcasses. I huffed and puffed as I pulled myself through the obstacle course for almost another kilometre.

Finally, I reached the top of the Khardung-La pass.

It was one of the highest motorable roads on the planet at an altitude of 18,380 feet, or 5,602 metres, almost 66 per cent of the height of Mount Everest!

I had cycled from Manali to Leh and from Leh to Khardung-La, covering over 550 kilometres on my cycle, crossing five high altitude passes all higher than 15,000 feet (4,500 metres), and riding through some challenging terrain and surfaces. I had prepared for over 18 months, logging thousands of kilometres on my cycle and doing multiple practice climbs in the lower Himalayan region (up to 9,000 feet, or 2,800 metres).

I was on top of the Khardung La Pass.

It felt great.

As I began my descent downhill to Leh, my mind went blank. I had spent the last 18 months planning, preparing, anticipating this epic cycle ride and now it was over! After the high, I felt empty, a loss of purpose in life. What next? What would I do now?

That evening Mausmi and I sat in one of our favourite open rooftop cafes along the mall road of Leh, sipping steaming hot ginger honey lemon tea and gazing at the tall, white peaks. The fading light was playing its last dramatics over their jagged surfaces.

I told Mausmi that I felt lost. She smiled and listened to me but didn't offer any solution.

The next day, we landed at New Delhi airport. Mausmi was taking a connecting flight to Kolkata. She had joined NIFT Kolkata as a professor after having done consulting work for apparel manufacturing factories all over Southeast Asia to improve their productivity. As we bade goodbye at the airport, she turned around and said, 'I think you should listen to your friends. I think you are ready to take the next step and begin a start-up.'

And that would happen on a lovely sunny winter afternoon when Mausmi and I went over to Abhishek's home for lunch.

On 26 January 2011, as India celebrated its sixty-second Republic Day, Abhishek, Mausmi and I gathered at Abhishek's place to feast on Mitali's famous rogan josh and pulao.

I had also asked Ganesh, a common friend, to join the meeting. I thought Ganesh could be a part of our start-up discussion. He had worked in my team in the past, and I felt he was a good tech guy, even though Abhishek did not think very highly of him.

Bratish was working in Kolkata for a Canadian start-up, and

I had decided to call him in the evening, depending on how things went. I was working in a US-based start-up as a Technical Architect and Mausmi had moved back from Kolkata to Noida, quitting her teaching job at NIFT.

Mausmi led the way that afternoon. Like a professor teaching her newbie students, she went through the problem statement that she had identified over her years of work in the global apparel industry. She can be a captivating and even a scary professor; you soon forget that she stands just five feet tall and weighs a measly 48 kilograms. We gathered around her with a cup of tea and listened.

She explained that the world had $1.5 trillion worth of apparel and fashion business.

This came from 10,000 global brands. Out of the 10,000 brands, about 500 were very large and recognizable names like Nike, Adidas and Gap. These brands got around 90 billion garments stitched every year and the garments were made in 500,000 factories worldwide, with 25,000 super-large factories mostly in Asia and South America. To stitch the 90 billion garments, these factories around the world bought around $300 billion worth of fabric. The fabric represented 70 per cent of the cost of the garments that we all wore.

She showed us how the fabric was used on the factory floor. We were taken aback to learn that almost 10 per cent of the fabric got wasted in the cutting process. It meant the world wasted $30 billion worth of fabric each year!

This leftover wasted fabric gets dumped into landfills, and the toxic chemicals from the fabric then enters the soil and the water table, contaminating both. In fact, the world over, garment production is the second-most polluting industry after the oil and gas industry aided by its emissions from all sources. It was unbelievable.

Then came the environmental impact of the wasted $30 billion worth of fabric. This cost the world 120 billion kilowatt hours' worth of energy or roughly enough to light the homes of 11 million households for a whole year. The wasted fabric also cost the world a whopping 200 billion litres of water, enough to fill 100,000 Olympic-sized swimming pools or fulfil the water needs of four million people for one whole year!

The question was why was there so much wastage? And could we do something about it?

Abhishek, Ganesh and I were wide-eyed, and we posed the same questions to Mausmi.

The wastage came from two major sources, she explained.

First, most factories around the world do their fabric planning through manual processes. They have some experienced professionals called cutting managers, most of whom have received a high-school level of education, and they do the plans on spreadsheets or papers. This archaic spreadsheet-based planning make the process poorly optimized, and thus the wastages creep in.

Second, the problem of cutting and planning was complex. Imagine if you had to plan a driving route from the Delhi Airport to Parliament. You would look for all possible parallel routes and choose the best. Google Maps does this for you, and you can rely on it each time.

This simple step of comparing parallel paths poses some serious challenges for apparel factories. A simple order with three sizes, say small, medium and large, and just five fabric rolls have 15,000 combined possible parallel paths. If dealing with 10 sizes and say 20 fabric rolls – an average-sized order for the industry – there would be over 10 trillion parallel paths to choose from.

We would have to build a Google Maps equivalent for apparel manufacturing processes. As the afternoon turned into a chilly evening, we couldn't stop talking about how we could solve this. We agreed that there was a large market with a pain point. If we could come up with a technology solution that could find the best manufacturing path, we could enrich the manufacturers and they, in turn, wouldn't have an issue paying for the service. On paper, the minimum sufficiency conditions for building a business were being satisfied. We agreed that we should build our start-up to solve this problem.

It was an exciting evening. We were all pumped up. We decided we would start our work in stealth mode and moonlight our way through building the Minimum Viable Product (MVP) for the moment – basically do our day jobs and work the evenings at my place or Abhishek's and effectively have two jobs for now.

We decided Abhishek would build the User Interface (UI) design and Ganesh the application tier code. I had to build the algorithms that would eventually plug the wastes. Mausmi had to do an in-depth industry study and get talking to her industry friends to see how we could engage with potential customers. I also had to call Bratish to let him know about these decisions.

At the dinner table, as we hungrily ate the fragrant pulao and the saffron-flavoured, delicately spiced rogan josh, Abhishek looked the happiest. He had been trying to seed this idea into our heads for a while now. Finally, it looked like it was happening.

After dinner, we chatted some more about what we would call the company and the product. It was the first major stumbling block! All the names we came up with were either already taken (that means .com domains were not available) or were available but for a steep price. After 90 minutes of frantic searching and arguing, we ended up with two names. We would call the product IntelloCut and the company ThreadSol (pronounced: threads all). Abhishek booked both the .com domains immediately.

We left around 10 p.m., having spent almost half the day in intense discussions. I called Bratish that night and updated him. He was also excited but was restrained, as he tends to be.

As Mausmi and I were preparing to go to bed, our phones hummed the notification tune.

There was one unread email from Abhishek@threadsol.com to our new ThreadSol email IDs. It read:

> Hello Everyone,
>
> I have created this new group so that we can communicate easily.
>
> Thanks,
>
> Abhi

I wish Abhishek had written something more dramatic – more representative of the momentous occasion. But the simplicity of the message meant that I remember it even today.

~

I sometimes think that we must have been high on drugs that afternoon.

We had not done even the most basic due diligence. Today, when I write this, I cannot help but think that we were reckless and hopelessly romantic to have taken this step.

Let me show you how ill-prepared and ill-informed we were and, just for the fun of it, let me do it in typical Bratish style – point by point:

1. We had not done the basic market sizing. We did know the overall scale of the fashion industry (90 billion garments, 25,000 large factories, $300 billion of fabric buy, 10 per cent wastage), but we didn't know where these large factories were and how much they were willing to pay. So, we didn't know what the revenue potential of our idea could be. Was it $1 million, $100 million, $1 billion?

2. We had no upper-echelon contacts in the industry. None of us had any sales background. We thought we could beat that. We thought the awesomeness of our innovation would carry us. This was madness!
3. We didn't know anyone in the upper echelons of the VC industry. The VCs put money into your enterprise and, in return, take up shares and, therefore, part ownership of the business. To get to them, you need contacts. We had none – nada, zip, zero! And yet, we thought we could raise money from VCs because our product would convince them! How juvenile!
4. We knew little about building a company and the legalities of doing our own business. We barely understood our income taxation, and if anyone asked us about what a balance sheet or a profit and loss statement was or what kind of EBIDTA (profit) margin we planned to build, we would have been skittled.
5. Finally, we didn't have any money of our own. It meant we could not sustain a dry period of no customer money or investments.

With start-ups, 90 per cent fail within the first three years and about 1 per cent end up being acquired or going to the Initial Public Offering (IPO) phase. These are the ones that are best prepared, most seasoned and most experienced. The art of building a start-up is not what we know from the stories of people like Mark Zuckerberg or Steve Jobs. They are the exceptional outliers. The run-of-the-mill entrepreneur must fight a hell lot more to get a functional founding team, build a MVP, raise money, get customers, grow the business . . .

It's a grind that only the very best survive. It is a good idea to know the answers to the five questions, without which it is plain suicide!

If I had met my younger self that night, I would have probably talked some sense to him. I would have told him the odds are stupendously great. And he does not have enough cards up his sleeve to make it work.

You should go home, son – who in the right mind would do this?

But perhaps, that's how our world is.

Innovators and explorers have time and again put themselves in harm's way and pushed the envelope to test their hypotheses.

Edward Jenner tested the smallpox vaccine on himself as he would not find anyone willing to try a test solution of muted virus serum of the deadly pathogen.

Joshua Kim circumnavigated the planet's oceans on his dinghy, *The Spray*, in 1896, much before the radio and GPS were invented! He sailed solo. And he didn't know how to swim!

There are countless examples of such heroics. And countless examples of heartbreaks and failures.

The story I am writing is nowhere as dramatic as those stories.

But the contours are the same. You need rational thought to innovate and irrational thought that you can make a change, and then try and reconcile the rational with the irrational. Entrepreneurship is not common. It seeks to tie romance with reason – it needs conflict and comfort.

When we began the journey of our start-up, it was with romance.

And as we know – romance doesn't last long!

4

Romance Doesn't Last Long!

I knew all about start-up shutdowns. I first experienced it in 1988 – when I was just eight years old!

It played out in the big and resplendent room of my school's principal.

It was a grand old room with high ceilings and a single desultory fan. It had a big mahogany desk with a giant globe on it, papers and files strewn around and a massive leather chair. Behind the desk was a cabinet of gargantuan proportions. All the awards that St Xavier's High School at Patna had won since its establishment in 1942 were on display.

And then there was the most dreaded object in the room. Beside the large leather chair was a plastic basket where a polished cane rested. It was the cane of fury, justice and discipline that all the 1,200 Xaverians feared. The hand that wielded it – our principal Father George Manimaala – was a legend. A call to his room was bad news, and the bravest young miscreants would go weak in their knee entering the massive room. And there I was being summoned to that dreaded room. I had broken the law and judgment was upon me.

So, what was my transgression? I knew many students in my school liked reading stories and comic books. Many of them saved their meagre pocket money to buy these books. I had also noticed that the six-monthly school magazine, *The Xavier Life*, was not able to capture the imagination of the students.

So, at the age of eight – in Class 3 – I forged a partnership with a friend, Amitash, and the two of us decided to start our handwritten magazine.

We debuted in April 1988, with four identical copies of 12 pages of poetry, stories and puzzles. We had worked for a week and prepared the contents. We had taken turns to write two manuscripts each. We had priced them at ₹1 for each copy (adjusting for inflation, it would be ₹30 today = $0.4). When Amitash and I announced our small little enterprise to our class, we were anxious. How would our classmates take this? Would they like it? Would anyone pay for our stories and poems?

In 45 minutes, we were all sold! We had made ₹4!

It was unbelievable!

We went to the ice cream vendor in the school and treated ourselves to a chocolate bar.

Amitash and I sat in the warm sun, nibbling the chocolate bar studded with nuts and raisins not quite believing our success. We laughed and agreed that it was the best chocolate bar we had ever had. Well, success does taste sweet!

In the next four months, we went from strength to strength. In the hay days, we were selling 40 copies a month. We had paid students to copy our original manuscript to make 40 copies (we never gave anyone the whole story or poem to save our intellectual property) and we were selling to the whole junior school! All the students and teachers knew about our start-up.

And we were rich and famous. We were eating ice creams and chaat when we wanted, as wide-eyed students all around asked us when the next issue would hit the stands. It was a dream run. And then it came to an abrupt screeching halt.

Amitash was absent from school that day and I was alone to face the sinister cane of justice. The meeting with the principal was swift and savage. George Manimaala spoke in a thick Keralite accent but he was crystal clear in his message. I was told that we were to stop the nonsense immediately. It was over. The regulatory authority had used its long hands to stop me from my first start-up!

And so I learnt that bitter lesson, all too early – that romances don't last long!

By spring 2011, we had all settled into a nice rhythm. We would all do our eight hours of office work from 10 a.m. to 6 p.m. and then meet at Abhishek's or my place at 9 p.m. and work until 3 a.m.

Weekends were marked for attending classroom training in fashion industry and garment manufacturing at Professor Mausmi's class. She would give us assignments and tests. It was hard going.

We had to understand the industry before we could write any tech to solve their problems. The schedule was gruelling. Six months on, we seemed to be getting somewhere. We had started to understand the industry and recognize its terms and jargons. And that's about the time when our first crisis came calling.

One Friday evening, Abhishek called me and told me that he wanted to come over to my place and he needed a 'talk'. He came in like a steam engine, bellowing smoke.

He was very disappointed and frustrated with Ganesh's work. The work was frequently incomplete and riddled with holes. Abhishek was getting stuck at his work because of Ganesh's non-performance.Mausmi and I had been harbouring similar suspicions. He was the slowest mover in Mausmi's weekend classes and was running behind in all assignments. I had also seen far too many bad work examples myself.

So far, I had defended Ganesh as I always thought he was a good tech guy and would turn around eventually. But even my patience was being tested. We were all putting 16 hours a day at work and couldn't afford a freeloader.

'Okay, let's pull the plug,' I said to Abhishek, 'let's stop all his access to mails, code and docs. We will meet him on Monday evening and cut him loose.'

Abhishek did what I said.

On Monday evening, I asked Ganesh to see me and Abhishek. I was very fidgety. Ganesh and I had worked together for many years. He had played important roles in my stage plays during my Impetus days. We had taken many trips together. We had shared so many memories and laughs together. This was stressful.

As Ganesh came into the room, I think he realized what was going to happen.

'Ganesh, as of this moment, you are not a part of ThreadSol anymore.' I said to him as Abhishek looked at his bootlaces. Ganesh looked at me and I felt our years of camaraderie melt away under his burning gaze.

'Do you want to say anything?' I asked.

He looked at me for a good five seconds and then said, 'No.'

Then he got up and walked out of the room. We didn't say goodbye and Ganesh has not spoken to me since. ThreadSol was on, but I had just lost a friend.

While losing a friend hurt me, I don't think I had much of a choice. Start-ups cannot afford a loss of focus and commitment. When you do not have a lot of money and nobody is giving you any elbow room, it is focus and commitment that takes you through.

The biggest reason for start-ups failing is founders falling out.

I think we nipped the issue in the bud at the right time. It would certainly not be the last time I would fire a close friend resulting in them never speaking to me again. I bear this cross; and I bear it for life. If only I could tell them that it pained me just as much. And it was never personal. I wish that we could have remained friends.

Indeed, romance doesn't last long.

But hope is an important ingredient of building a start-up. And your hope goes up with the small wins you get in the early days. These small wins make you think, *hey, it is all going well!*

5

Hey, It Is All Going Well!

By September 2012, about a year and a half after we set up, IntelloCut's MVP was ready. It took Mausmi, Abhishek, Bratish and I a full 18 months to come up with the first version. You could log in to our online solution and give it the manufacturing order information and IntelloCut would find the most optimized solution that could save the most amount of fabric.

Mausmi had quit her job but the rest of us were holding on to our day jobs. I think if we had quit our jobs and delved into this full time, we could have built the MVP in six months – but none of us had any savings to run our families, so we had to manage things like that.

It was a lot of fun, nonetheless. Mostly we would congregate at Abhishek's place around dinner time. We would have dinner together and sit around his table and work till late at night, sometimes pulling all-nighters.

Abhishek is a lot of fun to work with. After an hour's work, he needs a 15-minute breather. He would play cheesy Bhojpuri songs on YouTube – mostly to spite Mausmi and Bratish.

Abhishek and I would gang up on them and tease them with innuendo-filled cheap-sounding songs. Bratish and

We work days and we work nights
Mostly fun – barring some fights…

Mausmi, being more reserved, would shake their heads and feign disgust. Every 90 minutes or so, Mitali would bring us hot tea. Abhishek and I would take our tea and enjoy a cigarette on the balcony. Typically we would wind up by 4 a.m., and Mausmi and I would drive back home.

Bratish had an apartment, but I think he never spent a night there. He was also very sensitive to the cold. Born and brought up in Kolkata, the Delhi winter became his nemesis.

As the winter approached, he and Mausmi would move their work chairs near the hot air blower – all the more reason for Abhishek and me to gang up on them! Then in peak Delhi winter, Bratish ditched the chair completely. He would sit on the bed, throw a blanket over himself and work under that warm, dark, claustrophobic cocoon. He would stick his head out only to sip hot tea and duck back in.

As the nights went by, we kept taking one step at a time. Mausmi was our sounding board and she would greenlight our efforts if they were 'up to her high standards'. There were many rounds of re-dos and can-do-betters, and we kept the work going. It was intense – but it was a lot of fun. We were enjoying ourselves.

On weekends, we would engage in some important discussions.

How did we see this company being built?

How would we sell and reach the customers?

How will we prove value to the customers?

Do we think we are building a good product?

When do we see ourselves quitting our day jobs and running full time?

How would we scale the team?

How would we raise money from investors?

How do we reach the investors?

Who can help us?

There were too many questions and too many unknowns. One very important question was – who should be our first target customer? Mausmi thought we were better off focusing on the Delhi region's apparel manufacturing factories. She thought we should start with the small and medium factories and sharpen the product based on that feedback and then aspire to get the bigger ones like Madura Garments (Aditya Birla Group), Arvind Fashions, Raymond and Blackberry.

It made perfect sense – go to the small ones first and then land the big ones. But then, that's not how things would turn out. We had no clue that we were going to be thrown into the deep end of the pool right at the start.

Another question was, how would we raise money? In 2012, the start-up fever in India was rising and funding stories were becoming regular. RedBus, Flipkart, etc. were rapidly catching big bucks from VC funding. Part of my job in the company was to find contacts in the VC world and convince them to invest in ThreadSol. The problem was, I didn't know any.

I thought I could look up the large VC funds online and show them the awesomeness of our innovation, and they would be happy to invest in something that had the potential to be a global business. It made perfect logical sense – go to big funds and then land the big investment.

We had good logical-sounding plans – It was all going good!

Mausmi looked at me with disbelief in her eyes. She had just got an email – it read:

Dear Mausmi,

We would like to meet you at the India Habitat Centre on Sept 7th, 2012.

Yours,

Lal Sudhakaran

Madura Garments - an Aditya Birla Company

Madura Garments in Bangalore is regarded as one of the best, if not the best garment manufacturing factory group in India. They have around seven factories and they manufacture for Van Heusen, Louis Philippe, Peter England, etc. and their in-house brand Pantaloons.

They are regarded as one of the most technologically advanced in India.

Lal Sudhakaran was the head of manufacturing then and an industry stalwart. He had read Mausmi's articles on *StitchWorld*, an apparel industry magazine, and had reached out to her to understand what we were doing. Our first industry contact came from one of India's biggest! So much for going small and then landing big!

On the agreed date, Mausmi and I found ourselves sitting on the sprawling lawn of India Habitat Centre with Lal and his second-in-command Devdas. Lal was a tall man in his late 40s. Devdas was short and looked instantly lovable. They went through IntelloCut and its functionalities in great detail and asked many questions. We had a 15-minute time slot and ended up talking for about 90 minutes.

In the end, Lal stood up and shook our hands.

'Why don't you guys come over to Bangalore for a few days, and we can see what your solution can do? This looks very innovative.'

That's it!

One of the best manufacturing factories in India had just

invited us because they found our solution innovative! As they left, Mausmi and I were tempted to break into an impromptu dance in the middle of the lawn. But then India Habitat Centre is not a place where you can shake a leg any time you wish, so we suppressed the urge and drove back to Noida to tell our friends. It looked like success was coming to us.

On 1 October 2012, Mausmi and I reached Bangalore, enduring a 30-hour train journey.

Yes, we didn't take a flight – we had to save cost, we were a start-up and frugality was the way to go. We went straight to the Madura Garments factory – a 1.5-hour car ride from central Bangalore. For me, it was very exciting. I had never been to an apparel manufacturing unit until then.

We spent a whole week in Madura. It was terrific. We ran over 50 orders of shirts, jackets and trousers with our software and in each run, we showed them that we saved fabric. In the end, we showed them that we could save them 1 per cent fabric cost and 14 per cent labour cost.

Madura garments had a fabric bill of $100 million per year (₹650 crore). ThreadSol's IntelloCut would save them $1 million (₹6.5 crore at that time) each year.

They asked for a trial account to do more tests for 60 days and asked us to come back in early December 2012 to ink a deal with them. Not only did Madura start a trial, but they also introduced us to India's biggest denim (jeans) manufacturer, Arvind Exports. We were now in touch with two of India's biggest apparel manufacturers. This felt like Saurav Ganguly's dream Test match debut in England in 1996 when in difficult seaming conditions he scored back-to-back centuries.

As Mausmi and I embarked on the 30-hour train journey back to New Delhi, we were radiating confidence.

Maybe we were world-class after all!

The romance was still on.

It was all going well!

~

Buoyed by the successful run of IntelloCut at Madura, I decided to quit my day job and plunge full time into ThreadSol. It was a difficult decision. Mausmi and I had about four months of reserve money in all our savings and we were paying two car loans and a home loan and for a rented apartment. The results in Madura clearly showed that it was time for me to jump into this full time. And so, at the end of October 2012, I quit my day job.

I won't lie to you – it was scary to know that neither of us was earning. Sometimes, I would get this terrific paralyzing fear of what would happen when we ran out of money. Sometimes, the demons in my head would not let me sleep, and I would pace up and down the terrace the whole night, agitated by thoughts of impending doom. My parents were concerned. No one in our family had ever run a business or seen success in running their own endeavours. They worried that soon Mausmi and I would be back in Patna, empty-handed, soulless and jobless. Perhaps my parents had even made up a story that they would tell their folks that we were preparing for UPSC – otherwise, how would they explain us moving back to Patna to live with them? On the surface, they were supportive. Yet on the inside, they were scared, and so was I.

But then I would look at the results we were getting at Arvind. Arvind had sent us some 50 orders' data in a huge bulky courier, and we had chewed through it. We were looking to save them 3 per cent fabric, which would save them over $5 million a year.

That's huge!

Anyone who can save this much cannot have a bleak future,

right? These positives would slay the demons in my head and replace them with hope and optimism.

I guess this bipolar thought process is a part of every entrepreneur. It is common to experience abject hopelessness and boundless optimism all by the time you finish your morning tea.

Eventually, you adjust your emotions and concentrate on your job.

But it was not easy. Those first 14 days after quitting my job, I had major concentration issues. I was used to the routines of a day job, and this new reality was disorientating. I had to work hard to find a rhythm of working from home full time.

Meanwhile, I was spending a lot of time on LinkedIn and the websites of the VC funds of India and emailing them about our innovations. I was hoping that some of them would grant me a meeting. But I was not getting any positive responses.

Then I recalled that one of my cycling buddies Ashish in Bangalore ran a very interesting start-up platform named UnPluggd. They invited start-up pitches. They would then put 10 start-ups on the stand every six months in a very high-quality conclave that all the major investors, VCs, industry experts, start-up afficionados, wannabe entrepreneurs, glitterati entrepreneurs, students, media, etc. would attend.

So, ThreadSol applied for the UnPluggd 2012 December edition. Finally, we heard from Ashish.

Dear Manasij,

Happy to inform you that ThreadSol will be on stage on Dec 2nd 2012 for UnPluggd.

Congratulations.

Regards,

Ashish

Yep, we were in.

Mausmi and I were again going to Bangalore in December 2012. This time we were showcasing our innovation in one of India's biggest start-up events that would put us firmly in the crosshairs of the VCs, and we would be sitting with Madura for a discussion on commercials for our first sale. We were all overjoyed and excited.

Hey, it was all going good!

~

In the 1670s, the Dutch cloth merchant and a hobbyist lens maker, Antonie van Leeuwenhoek built a powerful lens that allowed humans to see microbes – amoebae, red blood cells, sperm cells – for the first time.

He wrote a manuscript with detailed diagrams and sent it to the Royal Society of London.

At that time, Robert Hooke was the guy to go to for anything about the world of microorganisms in London. He studied Leuwenhoek's manuscript and tried to replicate the observations.

He failed.

The world's tallest authority on microorganisms, who was employed in the world's most premier scientific organization, had failed to see what an obscure hobbyist in Amsterdam had!

Robert Hooke wrote one of the most remarkable reports about an innovation that he didn't understand. In a letter to the Royal Society dated 5 October 1677, he essentially declared that even after two–three days, he had been unable to see any tiny living things that Mr Antonie van Leeuwenhoek had claimed to see. He, therefore, concluded that either the apparatus he was using did not have enough magnification, or that the tiny living things mentioned by Leeuwenhoek thrived only in Amsterdam and not in London.

No, he didn't write off Antonie van Leeuwenhoek and his work. After his initial misgivings, Robert Hooke did confirm Leeuwenhoek's observations and reported the news of the Dutchman's success to the Royal Society.

Eventually, Antonie van Leeuwenhoek was credited with discovering the microscope, thanks to Robert Hooke and a few enterprising investors of the times. All the who's who of Europe, including the kings of England and Russia, made a beeline to his house to see the tiny world of Mr Leeuwenhoek. What a story!

Any innovation needs three things to happen.

Number 1: It needs an innovator to innovate.

Number 2: It needs a few early adopters (customers) to adopt the innovation and give it a shot.

Number 3: It needs a few backers who will back you with their money (investors).

We were good at number 1.

We were in search of numbers 2 and 3.

There was no way for us to know that this search was going to be painful.

How much pain would that be?

A world of pain!

6

A World of Pain

The meeting room had large glass walls. There were a dozen chairs neatly arranged around the large oval-shaped light-coloured wooden table. The early December afternoon sun shone brilliantly through the windows.

Mausmi and I sat in the room waiting for Madura's executives to come in.

We had sent them the proposal for IntelloCut to be deployed at seven of their factories. Based on all the trials, we had conclusive evidence that we could save them 1 per cent fabric and that would mean Madura would save \$1 million (₹6.5 crore) per year. We had sent them a proposal for seven plants to use intelloCut, and that would cost them \$150,000 (₹1 crore) one time to buy the licenses and \$22,000 (₹13 lakh) as yearly subscription charges.

Their seven plants could use IntelloCut from our cloud-hosted servers. In 2012, SaaS-based monthly subscription charges were almost unheard of for the apparel industry. The proposal was strong and had good logic. They would save six times the price of the product first year and 40 times the price of the product from year two. This was a great return on investment.

The meeting began with squeals of laughter at our price point. Apparently, they were amused that a start-up had the gumption to quote one crore to Madura for a 'software'. The executives made snide comments on the usefulness of our software for its price point. It did not feel good. The meeting was falling apart. Finally, they offered a number. $15,000 (₹10 lakh) for all seven sites and $1,500 (₹1 lakh) as maintenance charges from year two – a tenth of what we had quoted!

This was a blow. We had spent a lot of time at Madura. We had run numerous orders for them and they had verified the results. And now, after all the effort and time, these guys were offering us nothing but a dead rat on a stick!

Mausmi and I called for a break in the meeting. We needed to discuss our situation. And the situation was not very good; actually, it was quite grim – we had savings money in the bank that could keep us afloat for another two months – three if we really stretched it. The money these guys were offering would keep us going for almost a year, if not more. The temptation to say yes to their lowball offer was huge. We quickly discussed what we should do and came back to the meeting room.

'So, what do you guys want to do?' Lal asked.

'Well, frankly speaking, this offer is humiliating', I told him.

'Yes, I agree. But this is what we are offering,' Lal said. I liked him for his candour.

'We have a counteroffer. Why don't you guys use our software for free for the next six months? All we ask in return is Madura should give us flight tickets to come to Bangalore and assess the progress each month, and we should be able to bring folks from other factories over to show how Madura is using our solution and showcase Madura as a customer of IntelloCut. This will be all free. After six months, when you have accrued enough savings and you believe in this more, then you buy us for the price we are asking.'

I finished and looked around for their reaction.

They discussed my proposal among themselves and agreed. This was better than what they had thought.

They could enjoy the product for six months for free, and all they had to do was pay for our flight tickets and stay in the city – hell, yes!

We shook hands and left. We had Madura as our first customer – at least we could say that to the world and bring them over to see the software in action.

Finally, since we didn't agree to their price points, we hadn't jeopardized our prospects of getting the right price the next time from them or someone else. Accepting a low offer would have killed the price-point discovery. And we had won their admiration for being able to say no to Madura – something they were not accustomed to as most service providers bent over backwards to please the giant. It looked like a good tactical win.

However, I was conflicted. I knew I had gambled with our staying power in the game.

When I was signing this agreement, I didn't have any visibility of how we would remain afloat for the next six months – there was no money to last us that long!

As we were leaving, one of their executives told me that I was crazy to expect a price point of $22,000 per factory for IntelloCut (that's how we got to the number of $150,000 for seven). He said our price point was wrong and that we should revise it.

'I can bet,' he said, 'you guys are not going to get $22,000 per factory for this software.'

He was right. $22,000 per factory would turn out to be the wrong price point for our software.

In the next two years or so, we were selling IntelloCut for almost $60,000 per factory. I should have accepted his wager.

The Madura quasi-win was important for us. In the next six months, we worked like mules for them and posted one successful result after another. We trained their people, ran the software, helped them streamline their processes, spent countless hours on the floor, so much so that Abhishek, Mausmi and I didn't go for Bratish's wedding in early 2013 because we were in Bangalore instead. We had photographic evidence of our fabric savings and hundreds of reports testifying the benefits.

After six months, we had everything to make our case.

Great results? Check.

Well-trained team? Check.

Great support from our side? Check.

In May 2013, out of the blue, I received an email from Lal.

Hi Manasij,

We have decided not to go ahead with IntelloCut.

We have other priorities now.

Thanks for your efforts and all the best.

Regards,

Lal

And that's it.

They were gone.

They didn't return our emails, text messages or calls.

Someone told me that it was internal politics between two manufacturing directors that had drowned our prospects. Someone said that the management was now chasing the next shiny thing and we should have done the deal when we had their full attention. Someone said that our price point was way beyond what they could afford. Someone said that our product was not good enough. Someone said our after-sales product support was bad. We were handed many stories and many reasons.

Nonetheless, it was devastating. The world has no obligation to be nice to you and your innovation. This is your albatross around your neck. We knew this – but it still sucked. We had worked so hard and we had been thrown out like rag dolls.

We writhed in pain.

By the end of December 2012, Mausmi and I had gone through most of our savings. I got a fright every time I looked at the account statement and divided that with the monthly expense of our establishment. We were staring at the barrel of a gun. Another six weeks and we would be completely bankrupt. It was a scary feeling.

That's when we got our first break.

A common friend, Ashish Dahiya, who was especially close to Abhishek, invested ₹30 lakh into our business. Bratish and Abhishek, who were still working, also put all their savings into the business. This gave us a lifeline to run all our three families and the company for the next 10 months.

Abhishek and Bratish both quit their jobs in early 2013. All four of us were now working full time for ThreadSol. We had no fixed salary but access to the common funds, which we would use to pay for our household expenses. There were no vacations, no weekend breaks, no impulse buying, no eating out, no movie outings . . .

So much so that when Bratish took out his newlywed wife to dinner at Yo! China, he sent us a message later: '940 Rupees spent on Birthday Dinner ☹.'

Around the same time, we made our first hire.

Jaya was Mausmi's cousin. She stayed at our place and worked as a content writer and graphic designer. She would help us regularly with the tedious factory data analysis, and we decided to hire her and pay her ₹15,000 ($250) per month. Her biggest asset was her perseverance and hard work. Although she had no background in the software or apparel industry, Jaya would become one of the rock stars of ThreadSol and eventually emerge as one of the tall leaders in the business, delivering projects and customer success in over 16 countries!

Jaya and the four of us spent the first half of 2013 doing a crazy number of factory trials. The drill was painful and long.

Step 1: We would contact a factory owner. Most would never respond to emails. I had a rule of writing 12 emails to the same person over six weeks before I would declare them as 'unresponsive to solicitation'. Some of them haven't responded to date!

Step 2: We would present our software demo to them. Most of them closed the door on us at this step. The Delhi region is old school when it comes to adopting tech. The owners were the decision-makers, especially for the price point we quoted, but they didn't have the depth of technical understanding. Many meetings ended at the owner's desk.

Step 3: If the owner liked or felt intrigued by the prospect, they would ask us to liaise with their fabric-cutting manager and we would end up trying to convince someone who saw our software as an existential threat. They thought that if they went back to their owner with the news that the software was, in fact, making savings, it would paint them in a bad light in front of their bosses. So, many meetings ended with the cutting manager throwing cold water on the engagement.

Step 4: If the cutting manager liked the solution and was not insecure, they would usually tell us point-blank that there was no way a software could be smarter than them. Then they would challenge us to a duel! They would put in all their resources, experience, knowledge and skill and come up with a number on fabric consumption – something they thought their factory would consume to complete the fabric-cutting process for that specific order. We had to then plan the same order with our software and show that we could do that with less fabric.

This confrontational approach meant we had to endure a lot of nonsense on the factory floor. Convincing people was a hard task – despite clear instances of evidence. Sometimes, we would have to spend 10 days in a factory to run an order to show the value.

We had to endure everything from downright stupidity to dirty sabotaging. Most of this happened when we left the factory in the evening. When we came back in the morning, the world would have turned. You would not find fabric rolls, pieces would go missing, the order would be cut in the night citing urgent shipment needs and so on.

In many cases, we had to do 24-hour vigils to guarantee no one sabotaged the run.

Sometimes, after we spent 10 days and nights, we had the savings and photo evidence of the physically saved fabric, they would just trot along and change the initial target numbers to show that there were no savings! We would watch in disbelief while the triumphant cutting manager would smile and laugh at us along with his team. We would squirm and curse in our heads and sometimes express our anguish – but we all knew our effort was not going to deliver a thing.

If we cleared all the above steps and, on rare occasions, got the support of the cutting manager, we entered the final step.

Step 5: This was the final step of price negotiations. If you have not done price negotiations in the traditional 'Lala companies' (family-owned old businesses) in Delhi, you probably have no idea how bestial the experience is.

These guys are seasoned campaigners. They would sit coolly and use all the techniques to gain the upper hand. The modus operandi was the same. They would laugh, scorn, humiliate, sneer and abuse you while the owner's pets would sit around and join in tormenting you. If you lost your cool – good for them – they win. The deal was off. All we had to do was not lose our nerve, keep smiling and keep negotiating. It was not uncommon that our quote of $22,000 per factory used to be met with a counteroffer of $2,000!

On one occasion, while we were negotiating, a worker entered to serve tea. The owner rudely told the worker, 'Who told you to serve them tea?' On another occasion, we came for negotiation in the factory after a hard-fought bitter victory in the duel. I saw the owner's Porsche Cayenne parked in the driveway, gleaming in the sunlight. To break the ice, I said, 'I just saw your lovely car.'

The guy retorted, 'Don't think that just because I own a nice car, I will pay you more money.'

My jaw dropped to the floor. Did he just think I was a Hollywood Hills hooker and would name my price by looking at his car? All we could do was throw a laughing fit at his tasteless joke.

On another occasion, another lala told us, 'I agree on the savings, but I will not pay you this much because you are not white.'

We were dumbfounded.

Take your freaking savings and run dude. How does it matter if I am Asian, Caucasian or Alsatian?

Of course, I thought this in my head while I smiled and absorbed the rich racist's rants.

By the middle of 2013, we had done live factory trials in over 50 different factories in Delhi, Noida, Gurgaon, Faridabad, Bangalore, Tirupur, Surat, Ahmedabad and Ludhiana.

In every factory, the software passed with flying colours, and we could get clear, demonstrable savings. We were very confident that our tech worked well. It showed results for all kinds of garments – shirts, trousers, denims, dresses, lingerie, sportswear, outerwear, jackets.

Yet, all we had to show in the end was humiliation and ridicule. There were no sales. We had spent 300 days in 50 factories, where we worked flat out doing these customer trials, yet we caught no breaks!

Our money could last five more months. I could sense tension creeping into everyone's minds. If we could hit results in every factory, why were we not selling?

What was wrong with us?

What would it take us to get this noose off our necks?

The questions played in my head while I paced restlessly on my terrace in the warm summer nights.

'When would this world of pain end?'

Answer?

In three weeks.

We were about to hit a winning streak.

7

The Winning Streak

You may not know this, but Sir Frank Whittle changed your life forever.

In 1928, he was an audacious pilot in UK's Royal Air Force (RAF). Those were the golden days when planes had propellers. Whittle believed that planes needed to be faster – much faster. He came up with the design of the jet engine but the reception to his ideas wasn't positive. He was ridiculed openly by the RAF and Air Ministry.

The UK finally woke up to Whittle's ideas in 1939 when World War II broke out and Germany flew their first jet plane. The RAF was now willing to invest in building jet engines if he could show that his test engine could run for 40 minutes. The test engine ran for 42 minutes before it flamed out. The RAF invested £100,000 into his engine and aviation was changed forever.

The question is, why would the investment condition be an arbitrary 40 minutes of running? Apparently, it used to take 40 minutes for RAF planes to go from London to Paris and that became the yardstick on which the future of aviation was judged. How would history have turned out if the engine had failed in 38 minutes? Or, if the condition had been to mimic the flight time from London to Berlin – a two-hour distance in those days on propeller planes?

Lesson?

Investors throw up arbitrary impediments to tech that they have never seen before. When we went to the world with Threadsol, the start-up world already had competent technology start-ups in many domains. There were start-ups in edutech (education tech), fintech (finance tech), ecom (E-commerce), food tech (food delivery tech), retail tech, ride-sharing tech, etc.

But there was no apparel tech – tech that powered making apparel. No one had seen anything like us before and that was not the best bet for investments. In the investment world, we were called the black swan – something that has never happened and therefore no predictions can be made about it.

When Mausmi and I presented at UnPluggd in Bangalore in December 2012, we were pretty much laughed out of the auditorium. The investors in attendance thought our tech was 'cute' – a euphemism for a college-science project that has no future. We got a few meetings here and there mostly with the low-ranking office bearers of the VC funds, but we could not make any real progress.

However, UnPluggd delivered us one very important connection. Seated among many start-up enthusiasts was a man named Gowtham from Microsoft. He was in charge of a start-up programme called the Microsoft Bizspark – a bold step by Microsoft to embrace the start-up ecosystem. He liked what he saw that day in UnPluggd.

In April 2013, I got a call from Gowtham. He said that Microsoft was doing a countrywide start-up challenge and that we should participate. First, we needed to apply to the Delhi regional chapter and then participate in a pitch day in Delhi. Similar pitches would happen in Mumbai, Kolkata, Pune, Hyderabad, Chennai, Kochi and Bangalore.

The best from each chapter would lock horns in Bangalore for the national final.

The winners would take home a lot of goodies and get almost $100,000 worth of software and cloud access from Microsoft Azure. But most importantly, it would open avenues to reach other investors.

So, we applied. And we got promptly rejected! I called Gowtham and told him what had happened. Gowtham went back to the screening committee and asked them to take another look at our material and this time, we got invited to the Delhi zone pitch day.

It was a bright summer morning when Jaya and I went to the Times Internet office in Noida's Film City. The place was buzzing with young founders. There were around 20 chosen start-ups. Each of them would get 10 minutes to pitch their innovation, and based on that the judges would crown the winners. Gowtham met me at the venue and said, 'Dude, don't screw up. I will look bad. Try to finish in the top 10 at least.' I knew he was under pressure.

When the judges announced the runners-up and then asked the gathering, 'Guess the winner?' The hall erupted with cheers of 'ThreadSol!' We were the best start-up in North India!

A few months later, we were in Bangalore at the national final. It was a big affair in the Microsoft Accelerator office on Lavelle Road, in the heart of Bangalore. As I reached the venue, the scale of the event became clear. There were hundreds of people, a large gathering of media, a big contingent of VCs, lots of start-up folks – it felt like a carnival. The stage was huge and there were screens placed in each aisle so that everyone could see the presentations. Everything was plush.

There were 10 of us finalists. Everyone was dressed up and

looking debonair in their jackets and tie. I had gone with a black-and-white combination – black trousers, white shirt, black waistcoat and a black tie. Funnily enough, all my competitors were also dressed in black and white. So, we all probably looked the same. We were all equally nervous, most of us were, no doubt, battling demons in our heads. Winning the final mattered and a lot was at stake.

Every presenter got 15 minutes and then five minutes for questions and answers. I was the sixth speaker – right in the middle of the jamboree. As I was waiting for my turn to come, I saw one CEO after another representing their start-up and delivering brilliant pitches. Their strong alpha performance made me nervous.

As the fifth presenter was talking, I got up and went to the wings. I remember, when I used to host a TV show in Doordarshan Patna in my school days, the director always told me that the best way to feel easy is to look at the camera and audience for a while before you go and read your lines. I gazed at the audience. The host of the show announced my name.

I felt a surge of nervous energy as I walked on to the stage with dazzling lights and whirring cameras. Fifteen minutes on the clock, slide changer in my hand, a hall full of audience, here we go . . .

'Gentlemen, Ladies . . . welcome to the biggest start-up beauty pageant show of India. I am pageant contestant number six – Manasij Ganguli, representing IntelloCut the product and ThreadSol the company . . .'

I have been on stage on numerous occasions in school, college and the companies I have worked for. I have hosted TV shows as a kid and been on TV and radio shows as a panelist. Public speaking came naturally to me and except for a few forgettable experiences, I have generally fared well on stage. I have never been very good with prepared speeches and, therefore, I never memorize and deliver lines. I always have a general map of what I want to say and then use situational inspirations, humour and story-telling to communicate my thoughts.

In fact, I can do a five-minute piece to a camera without a script, without a single stutter or stammer.

I think, my performance on the stage that day was impeccable. As I was wrapping up, I saw on the digital clock display that I had 60 seconds more. So, I added – 'We at ThreadSol and IntelloCut save fabric, cost and time for the manufacturers, just as I have saved 50 seconds in my talk today. That's a 5 per cent savings. Thanks a lot.'

There was a lot of applause as I ended.

Two hours later, I was holding the first runner-up trophy of the 2013 Microsoft BizSpark India Startup Challenge. We were declared the second-best start-up in India among a thousand applicants! There was a flurry of media interviews and thousands of handshakes. But most importantly, I ended up with around 50 business cards of India's top VC firm representatives.

I sometimes feel it is unfair that these start-up shows are designed to favour good speakers and presenters. In this case, I had a natural advantage but then it's entirely possible that a very high-quality innovation might be drowned just because they may not have a great presenter as their CEO. The game is not entirely fair. But, on that day, on that stage, we did win.

As I was going back to my sister-in-law's place in Bangalore, a place I usually bunked when in Bangalore, I got a call from Jaya. She was doing a live factory trial at Texport Industries, Bangalore and we were expecting a 4 per cent savings.

'We have a problem,' Jaya told me on the phone.

'We didn't get the savings?'

'No, we got the savings and I have clicked the saved fabric roll's pic.'

'Then what's the bloody problem?'

'These guys are unable to believe their eyes and they won't let us leave. They are cross-checking for the last hour and counting all the 1,700 pieces to confirm that we have completed the work. What do I do?'

I smiled and leaned back in the cab seat as it made its way through the mad Bangalore traffic.

No, we didn't win because of how I did on stage, we won because there is a factory that is unable to believe our awesome results. The tech was awesome. The tech won.

We were on a winning streak.

I shifted to Bangalore leaving Mausmi in Noida temporarily. Bangalore was hotting up as almost all my VC meetings were in Bangalore. Being the winners of the start-up challenge, I had a lot of meetings in the pipeline. There was also very good media coverage that kept the momentum on for us.

In the middle of all this, we had a big break. We did our first trade show in Noida. It was a small show and we had a booth with standees, brochures and lots of business cards. In that show, we met up with the CEO of a large manufacturing facility in Bahrain. He spoke to us for a long time and invited us to come to Bahrain to showcase our work at his factory.

This was super exciting. For the first time, we had received some international interest.

So, I landed in Bahrain in late June 2013 to do a three-day trial at their factory. Bahrain was super-hot and dusty. This was my first trip to the Middle East. The living quarters provided by the factory were very basic but I couldn't care less about the ambience and comfort.

I was kicked about being able to make an international run out of our start-up idea. I was also a bit nervous as we knew the group we are dealing with was a very famous one and had great people and systems. Would we be able to deliver the results on an international stage?

The factory had 24-hours production. It was super large and everything looked intense. People carried handheld radio devices for instant communication and frequently barked orders on the radio to each other. I was given a large order that I had to complete in two days and two nights. I spent those 48 hours on the factory floor and we ended with a huge 300-metre fabric roll saved! Thankfully they didn't make me wait while they counted all the 40,000 pieces in the order.

The deal negotiation went the Delhi way though. I came back to Bangalore empty-handed but with terrific confidence that even on an international stage, even when we are pitted against the best factories and the best systems, our innovation would win and deliver terrific results. My confidence in our innovation was higher than ever. ThreadSol's IntelloCut is a prospective global play – we might have an international business someday.

As I came back to Bangalore, I received an invitation to visit Shanghai. Every two years, Shanghai hosts the biggest apparel machinery and software trade show named CISMA. My invite came from the agents of Gerber – a US-based $1 billion machinery and software company that serves the apparel industry. They were interested to learn about our software. Now our start-up was going to China! And that too to meet a billion-dollar company interested in our innovation. This was awesome!

In the meantime, we had two more people join us after Jaya. Mausmi's old colleague Ankita was now working with us. She was looking at the customer trials with Jaya. Manisha also joined us. She was a long-time friend of Abhishek and mine. We had worked together in Impetus and she was handling marketing for us. She did a great job in milking the success of the Microsoft BizSpark start-up challenge and got us regular media mentions. With new people and more travel, our running costs were now higher than ever. We were still operating from my Noida home while I was staying at my sister-in-law's place in Bangalore.

Meantime, we had many promising investor meetings in Bangalore. Everyone was showing excitement about our solution, and there were promises for follow-up meetings with the bigger honchos for the final nod. So even though the customer end of the story was still frustrating, the mood was high. The wins in Bahrain and the Microsoft Bizspark start-up challenge turbocharged everyone.

'We will make it', we all believed.

It's funny that I didn't know that to make it big, you needed to throw caution to the wind . . .

The path ahead goes low and high
Alone and miserable in Shanghai…

8

Throw Caution to the Wind

Shanghai! September 2013

The megacity conjures up images of a glittering bund (the riverside), tall skyscrapers and the world's first maglev train – a true testament to the Chinese economic miracle.

For me, Shanghai was a super cheap hotel in the Pudong area ($30 per night). The room was so small that if I jumped from my bed, I could land on the toilet bowl. You need to know Chinese to be able to get by in cheap areas of Shanghai. English is alien. It took me 40 minutes to check into my room as the hotel clerk's English and my Mandarin were of equal proficiency.

Sign language works, but it calls for patience. It took me another hour to find the McDonald's for dinner as there was hardly anyone to help me find my way. Google Maps on VPN doesn't work and unless you have Baidu Maps (that runs in Mandarin), you are pretty much stuck.

Every two hours or so, there would be playing card-sized leaflets thrown under my door that had photographs of scantily clad Chinese women in suggestive poses. I was tempted to call the number because the leaflet said that the women spoke English and I needed help to get by! I spent the whole night tossing and turning, nervous about the meeting with Gerber.

CISMA was a mega trade fair. There were 10 indoor stadium-sized halls and thousands of exhibitors from all over the globe. Gerber had a big prominent stall and I was introduced to Bill and Mary from the company. They sat through my demo and asked decent questions but I realized that there would be no joy for us – they were simply not keyed up to risk their cozy corporate positions by sticking their neck out for a rookie start-up.

Gerber had many resellers and agents in all the countries. They took an immediate liking to our solution. I met the resellers from Bangladesh, the Philippines, Sri Lanka, Indonesia, Pakistan, etc. They introduced their local customers to me and I exchanged cards with them. I got invites to visit the Philippines and Turkey. I was enjoying myself and it seemed there could be a return on investment of this expensive trip after all.

Just as I had wrapped up speaking to three British guys from Adidas, I felt a tap on my shoulder. I turned around and found Bill standing behind me. He took two steps towards me, right up to my nose and said in a menacing tone, 'Mate, this is Gerber's stall, you understand? I am going to turn around and count to 10. And when I turn back, you are gone, right?'

'Yes sir,' I said.

As I walked out of the stall, I felt the blood rush to my face and ears and turn warm. The public humiliation and the rudeness was hard to bear. It's so easy to trample on a small insect, and Bill had just shown that we were nobodies and we could be easily squashed. This would not be my last meeting with him though.

Shanghai showed that we had international potential.

It also showed us that it would not be easy to come by.

Back in Bangalore, I narrowed down my investment pitches to angel investors and small investing groups. Our investment ask was ₹1 crore ($150,000). A quick primer on why we needed ₹1 crore. If you were a first-time founder in 2013 – ₹1 crore was the kind of money you could get at the very early stages (called seed round in start-up lingo). We estimated that with ₹1 crore, we could grow our business to a topline of ₹2–3 crore and then raise more to fund our subsequent growth. In any pitch for funding, the VCs are always looking at what the next round raise is and what the valuation could look like. That's the prime mover for any VC investment.

The large VCs simply didn't deal with small investments of ₹1 crore or so. They would meet us nonetheless to keep us in their mind in case later we became big enough for them to take us seriously. Most of the time, the large VC firm guys would connect us to smaller investment firms and HNIs (high net-worth individuals, or angel investors).

The angel investors were a tough breed. These are guys who are super-duper rich and they have more money than they can spend in their lifetime. The start-ups and their crazy valuations had made it a lucrative place to invest some money and diversify their investment portfolio. Most of the meetings were one-on-one and took place in opulent five stars or plush restaurants.

These meetings were not going very well. On one occasion, I was called to The Leela Bangalore for a breakfast meeting. The discussion was highly uninspiring, and I spent most of my time listening to a rich man ranting about the world. Suddenly, he got a call and he rushed out, excusing himself. On top of a disappointing meeting, I had to pay ₹5,000 ($90) as he had left the hotel without paying the bill.

On another occasion, a guy called us to meet at the patisserie of the Oberoi Grand in New Delhi.

We went there and ordered plain water with ice. Just asking for plain water seemed awkward and ordering it with ice looked like you did order something – without any liability for any payment coming your way.

My rich host sat down and called the waiter and said, 'Bring me my usual.' I had spent four years in an engineering college where I was a daily visitor to the dhaba and even there I could never say 'my usual'. In fact, there is not a single place on the planet where I could say 'my usual' and the guy would know what to bring, let alone at a five-star restaurant!

All the angel investor meetings ended on a similar note.

'I will invest if angel X invests or if you can find a lead investor, say ABC group.'

Then they would connect you with angel X and a smallish investment group ABC. Then you met angel X.

Angel X mostly ended the meeting with, 'I will invest if angel Y invests or if you can find a lead investor, say PQR group.' So, you met angel Y. And the cycle repeated.

I would also meet ABC and PQR – the smaller investment funds that invested at the seed fund stage – the same stage we were at.

Meanwhile, Microsoft did a great job introducing us to Harvard Angels and Bangalore Angels – angel investment groups. The meeting with the Bangalore Angels happened in the same hall where I had won the national start-up challenge. It was a gathering of 40-odd angel investors. I was again on the same stage. I delivered the same winning pitch again.

'This technology already exists,' some guy from the angel investor community said.

'Really? Who has it?' I asked.

'Oh, I had a Gerber machine and it had this technology 20

years back. I ran a garment factory as an owner. This chap is lying,' said the angel with a devilish laugh.

I tried to explain that we had just been called to Shanghai by Gerber to discuss our technology, and even if we concede that the tech already exists (which was false), the business proposition remained the same. After that, all hell broke loose. I was heckled off the stage.

After all the pitches were over, not a single angel investor came to speak to me. They looked at me as a con artist who had been exposed by the fearless activism of one of their super-wealthy colleagues. One of them came over and said, 'Maybe you should introspect as to why you still don't have a customer or an investor putting any money behind you.'

I thought these were very wise words. I did some hard introspection and came to the solemn realization that the buffet was a complete washout and the chicken 65 was cooked nowhere near to my liking. So, I decided to skip the snacks session and went home. A month ago, I had emerged triumphant from the same hall as one of the best start-ups of India. Today, I left the place humiliated and dejected. I had just been called a liar.

There was another angel investor group meeting the next day. I sent Manisha for that meeting and I went to talk to a customer. Manisha met a guy named Velu in that investor meeting. Velu told us that he would help us close a deal with an investor, but we would have to pay him 5 per cent of the amount raised. I agreed – but he would have to help me close the deal and the terms and not just make an introduction. He agreed. He also told me that I should expect some interest in the Mumbai Angels meet-up in Mumbai that was due in a few days.

I was planning to skip that meeting as I had now met over 30 VC groups and 50 angel investors. I was getting a feeling that this was not helping, and we may have a better chance at closing a customer deal than convincing a rich guy to drop a penny in our begging bowl.

Dealing with Velu was a mistake. I would realize this later.

Mumbai! September 2013

It was a rain-soaked day in Mumbai. I had taken a long-haul overnight bus from Bangalore to Mumbai – yes, we pulled all stops to save cost and the return trip on the bus was eight times cheaper than the flights.

I reached The Lalit in Mumbai – another five-star hotel – almost three hours before the start of the event. The venue was amazing. Mumbai Angels was the largest angel group in India with some 200+ members. The organizers were setting the place up. The main ballroom was set up for the start-up pitches. There were round tables draped in milk-white fabric, with name cards for the distinguished guests. Mineral water bottles with candies adorned every table. I didn't see a place for entrepreneurs though, but I didn't pay much attention either. I should have!

Later the five chosen companies and their entrepreneurs arrived – all looking sharp and smartly dressed. An attractive-looking young woman explained the rules of the engagement to us.

'Each of you will get 30 minutes to present and 15 minutes for questions and answers. While one entrepreneur is presenting, the others will wait outside.'

'Why?' I asked.

'Oh, we do not want your idea to be copied,' she said without skipping a beat.

'Really? You think I will abandon the last two years of work just because someone has a cute font on their presentation?' I didn't make any attempts to withhold my sarcasm.

'Well, let's ask the others.' She turned to the others.

To my horror, my fellow entrepreneurs agreed with the good lady.

We drew chits and I came up last.

Great!

'So, where do we wait?' I asked again.

'Over there.' She showed a narrow passageway right in front of the men's washroom.

'There are only two chairs . . .'

She looked at me with a blank stare, but I read her mind – 'Play musical chairs, you moron.'

I came out of the ballroom area and went to the garden smoking area. I felt really resentful being here.

'That's it. I am done being humiliated all the time. This is nonsense. I am not going to play the passive "let me try to please you always no matter what you say" guy anymore.'

It was time to throw caution to the wind.

I spent a lot of time in the garden. I opened my laptop and worked on my fabric-saving algorithm. Somehow, writing code always felt therapeutic. Code always behaves with logic and if your logic is right, the code will reward you. I liked the orderly world of logic-driven actions, and the world of computer codes was always a refuge that I found comforting.

By the time it was my turn to present, I had come up with a neat plan. I went into the resplendent ballroom. There were around a hundred people in that room. I had 30 minutes to do my presentation and I finished in 10 minutes flat!

'But you didn't tell us how you actually save this fabric?' Someone from the audience asked.

I took a dramatic pause and then said, 'I have been a fan of Mandrake the Magician as a kid. Whenever someone asked him how he performed a trick, Mandrake always said – magicians don't tell.'

I loved my answer. It was cocky as hell and I had no intention of giving an in-depth response to a bunch of guys with inheritance money who had nothing to do on a Saturday morning. The Q&A session unraveled quickly and was over in five minutes because I didn't give even one straight response. I had saved them 30 minutes!

It was lunchtime and afterwards the angels were free to mix with the five chosen entrepreneurs.

After my dream performance, I was assured that no one would ever touch me with a barge pole.

So, I loaded my plate with the excellent chicken chettinad and fried rice and sat in a quiet corner table and enjoyed my lunch. Post lunch, I went out for a quick smoke. As I was enjoying my cigarette, a big BMW 7 series drove up near the porch. I saw one of the marquee angel investors come out of the ballroom. He opened the rear door of the car and saw me and made a gesture to me to come towards him.

I walked up to his car.

He said, 'You know what's your problem?' He had his left foot inside the car already.

No I don't, but I bet you are going to tell me, I wanted to say. Instead, I said, 'Please, tell me.'

'Oh, you will get tired.' He said this and off he went.

Yes. I was tired of chasing investors. The last few interactions had made me realize that we might not get an investor's blessings for our kind of business and that I was done being a pushover.

Just as I was thinking about this, my phone rang. It was Mausmi.

'Hey, how is it going?' Mausmi asked.

'I feel like the old hooker on the street who is all decked up but has no date,' I said.

'Well, hang in there,' she said.

I decided that I would go back and thank the organizers before leaving. That would turn out to be a wise decision.

I was preparing to leave when someone called my name from behind, 'Do you think we could have a quick chat?' It was a guy in his forties with a deep voice. Our quick chat lasted almost an hour. For a change, I was talking to someone who would never interrupt me mid-sentence to put their views over mine.

This was my first meeting with Karthik. He ran Blume Ventures, India's most prolific early-stage investors. Karthik was genuine and sincere. I was cocky and jumpy in the first few minutes of the discussion but calmed down as our conversation progressed. We exchanged notes on our product, our seemingly unending number of successful customer trials without a deal and my frustrations with the angels and VCs in trying to raise money, with no solid commitments.

He was sympathetic and weighed in on the fundraising side. I didn't know where the conversation was going, but I liked his display of empathy and concern. He said that he liked what he heard from me about our innovation and he liked my attitude while I presented.

As he got up to leave, he patted my back and said, 'Well, I would like to invest in your business. I will put up 50 per cent of round money and the rest we will hustle with the angels. Now if you excuse me, I have to attend another meeting.'

I was stunned.

What just happened?

Was this serious?

I felt a terrific sense of relief. Yes, all this drudgery was somehow worth it! We had our first investment intent in our hands.

Wow!

I called my friends and everyone back home was overjoyed. It was the win everyone had been praying for.

I came out of the hotel and stood at a shanty tea stall. It began to rain really hard. As I stood under the tarp canopy sheltered from the rain and sipped a cup of sugary-syrupy tea, I felt 10 pounds lighter – as if someone had lifted a heavy load off my chest.

My overwhelming emotion that late afternoon was a heavy sense of relief. I have often looked back at that day and wondered why I didn't feel happy. I think it's because happiness comes when you get something unexpected or if something works as planned. For all those long tedious climbs, where you have fallen on your knees multiple times, reaching the chequered flag delivers firstly a sense of relief. Later, as you get more and more experienced at seeing results at the end of a long haul, the sense of relief gives you happiness. In that sense, entrepreneurship and its particular happiness is really an acquired taste.

That night I stayed wide awake on the 16-hour bus ride from Mumbai to Bangalore. My co-passenger snored away, going high, then low, then high again. On any other day, I would have been annoyed, but that night, I found this minor discomfort amusing.

It looked like we might be okay after all.

And we indeed came out okay.

But not before we almost died.

Yes, we had only 28 days to death!

9

28 Days to Death!

On a clear sunny day, the Taj Mahal is a sight to behold.

Every time I visit this monument, I just cannot imagine the scale of the enterprise that was undertaken to build it – and that too in an age when modern technology didn't exist.

There was no GPS to build such a huge building with its monster-sized courtyard where everything lines up and fits with perfect symmetry. There were no planes bringing architects and engineers from Persia (Iran) and Turkey; their journeys on horse-drawn caravans instead would have taken months. At the time when the Taj Mahal came up, it would have been almost 10 times taller than other buildings around it.

It was a bright early November afternoon with clear blue skies under a warm sun. We had a signed investment term sheet in our hands and buoyed by that, we had made a few more hires.

One of the angels Karthik had pulled in was Rajan Anandan, ex-managing director, Google India, and a marquee angel investor.

Blume's backing and Rajan's onboarding enthused other angels. Suddenly I had a deluge of calls from them, all eager to put in money. Even the Mumbai Angels came around with a few guys willing to put in the money.

This volte-face amused me. The angel investing world is led by a few alpha investors like Rajan. As soon as one of the alphas back a fledgling start-up, it creates a huge FOMO (fear of missing out) in the other angels and they start falling like ninepins to get on the same bus with the alpha.

Rajan and Blume had just shown the hungry angels where the next pot of gold was. Within two weeks, the round was fully subscribed – we had reached our target. Now I had to blow off the same folks who had blown me off a few months back.

With the promise of the ₹1 crore funding, we had hired two engineers – Santosh and Kamal, from BIT Mesra, Noida Campus. These guys were to help Abhishek and Bratish in building the IntelloCut software. We had also hired three people from NIFT, Delhi. We had picked Anas to help me with sales, Silky to help Mausmi, Jaya, Rohit and Ankita with customer trials and Nikita to help Manisha with marketing. We boarded a 12-seater bus and went to see the lovely Taj Mahal.

Fun story – ThreadSol has made only two offsite day trips to the Taj Mahal. This was the first – in November 2013, with 12 people. The next time would be five years later, in December 2018 with 120 people, just a day after ThreadSol was acquired! All the people who made the first trip would also be present on that last trip.

On our way back, as the bus cruised on the highway, we broke out into groups playing dumb charades. In the middle of this fun-filled atmosphere, I saw my WhatsApp explode with messages from Blume. It looked like we were likely to get the money in the bank in a few months, by the end of the year 2013 or the beginning of 2014.

This immediately concerned me. I forwarded the messages to the WhatsApp group of the founders. The moment they saw the message, I saw their faces turn white. Our burn rate had gone up now that we had more people. We had money that would only last us six weeks. The end-of-the-year timeline for funds to hit meant we were dangerously close to being bankrupt.

I saw the messages in the group:

Bratish: Do we have money to last that long?
Abhishek: I don't think so. Mausmi?
Mausmi: No, we cannot clear December 2013 end without funding.
Abhishek: What is the plan?
Bratish: Let's play, we cannot spook our folks now.

As I got up to enact the movie *A Wednesday*, I knew Bratish, Abhishek and Mausmi had their hearts in their mouth. So did I. For a moment, the whole set-up looked surreal to me. I am with a bunch of 20-year-olds who believe in us and the vision of ThreadSol. Here we were having fun while the four of us knew this might just come to an end in the next few weeks.

~

29!

That was the number of days in which ThreadSol would go bankrupt. Mausmi used to send a number each day to our founders' WhatsApp group. That was her way of saying good morning to us. This countdown added that extra bit of urgency to the start of each day. On that November morning, as I crawled out of the bed and looked at the phone, I felt a chill down my spine.

I was hearing horror stories of VC firms and angels promising money and not honouring them. I had met with entrepreneurs who would chuckle at our naivety in hiring people without having the money in the bank. 'You will get screwed dude, you will,' one of them had warned me and I was dreading this.

Karthik and Ashish from Blume kept a positive spirit and cheered me up each time we chatted.

'Don't worry, you will see the money before the year winds down,' they would say. However, the process was taking its time. I will be honest – I was getting more paranoid with each passing day. There was a lot of pressure. We all felt it. And Mausmi gave it a number each morning.

29! That's below the one-month mark!

As I was starting my day with a cup of aromatic Darjeeling tea, my phone hummed. It was from an unknown number. It read: 'Hi Munseez, I am Rajiv Jasuja from Formal Clothing Company, Bangalore. I have heard positive feedback from Madura about your software. Can you meet me? My office is in Basapur, near Electronic City, Bangalore.'

Munseez?

I am sure he meant Manasij. It's not unusual for people to spell and pronounce my name incorrectly. Except for a few close friends, no one gets my name right and certainly not at the first attempt.

Anyway, that afternoon I met Rajiv Jasuja. He was a man of medium build, in his early forties, and had a few strands of white hair. The factory was small and made only 800 shirts a day, and I was sure they wouldn't be able to afford our solution. I did my routine demo and had a long conversation with Rajiv. He asked me for a trial run of the product, and we decided that we would be doing the trial the very next day.

'Great, another trial.' As I left the factory and drove back, I was not very hopeful. We had done many trials already and all of them had been a dead end. Why would this be any different?

As I was thinking so, I got a call from Ashish, the CFO of Blume.

'Hey, Manasij. Are you in Bangalore tomorrow?' he asked.

'Yes. I am. But I will be in a factory where we are trialing,' I said.

'Ah great. I will come and see you there. I will also be able to see how your technology works and saves fabric in a live environment.'

I felt tense as I hung up.

Why does he want to meet in the factory?

Are they having second thoughts about the feasibility of our technology and want to check it out themselves?

Then I became angry at myself.

Why did I tell him about the factory trial?

We know how dishonest some factories have been – suppose we cannot show any savings?

Suppose Rajiv Jasuja and his folks don't give positive feedback?

Will Blume walk back on their promise of investing?

I only have 29 days.

As my car got stuck in an endless traffic signal at the Silk Board, I became increasingly uneasy and paranoid.

That evening we all gathered around the television in Manisha's flat. It was Sachin Tendulkar's last day as an international cricketer. We heard his farewell speech and I was moved. I have been a Sachin fan for a long time and I felt sad that I would never ever see him packing off the fast bowlers with his trademark straight drive. Sachin personified cricket for a generation of Indians, including me. At one point, I could count each of his centuries and rattle out the stats of his remarkable career. His farewell made me feel even more melancholic.

28!

Jaya and I reached the factory early in the morning. Rajiv Jasuja gave us a 700-piece shirt order from Thomas Pink – a high-quality men's shirting brand.

The order was very small and there were only five fabric rolls. Jaya and I got to work quickly.

I wanted to wrap up the order by 3 p.m. to show Ashish the saved fabric roll when he came to see me. I was tense. The margin was very slender and our software was projecting a 35-metre roll saving that would be around 6 per cent savings for this order. Every time a defective piece of fabric was found, I would get a jolt.

Damn, two metres in defect!

My savings are down to 33 metres now. I would cringe and squirm internally.

At 2.30 p.m., the on-floor execution came to an end. We had a 30-metre roll left as pure savings.

It was a win! Rajiv was happy and I was relieved.

At 3 p.m. Ashish came in. He went through the software process in brief and saw the physically saved roll and had a pleasant chat with Rajiv who gave him good feedback. Ashish was pleased.

'Chief, don't worry. You will have the money wired very soon.' He patted my back and left.

I heaved a sigh of relief.

I now had a final discussion with Rajiv. After our experience in other factories, I had low hopes from this one. Besides this factory was small, so I had my doubts about their purchase power.

Rajiv and I sat in a windowless room. It was small and kind of stuffy. I had the reports of the day's software run printed and neatly stacked on the table. He didn't touch any of the reports.

'So, to use your software, we need a computer with an internet connection. That's all?' He asked.

I was taken by surprise. So far, no one had started the meeting with this line of thought.

Was he actually contemplating using our software?

'Yes. All you need is an ordinary computer and then you can use the software from the cloud, just as you use Gmail, Facebook, etc.,' I replied.

"Okay, what is the price of your software?'

'Well, we sell this for $22,000 per site.'

'Hmm, that's like ₹13 lakh. Look Munseez, I cannot pay that much. I am a small factory but I would really like to use your software. Can you please accept a $15,000 price?' Rajiv looked visibly embarrassed as he quoted his price.

He put his number on the table and gazed downwards at his bootlaces. He thought I would blow him off for his lowballed offer.

On the other side of the table, I was unable to believe myself.

Is this finally going to happen?

Am I going to catch a break finally and have someone pay for our software?

My heart was beating so fast and so loud that I think Rajiv could hear it. I looked at him.

He was not the shrewd factory owner type – he was a progressive fellow who had his constraints and was still willing to bet on a start-up.

'Let's do this.' I extended my open palm, and we shook hands warmly and smiled. In the next 30 minutes, we signed the agreement, and Rajiv mentioned that he would have the money wired to us by the close of the business.

It started raining as I left the factory. It was around 6.30 p.m., and it was dark and getting cold.

I had a myriad of emotions playing on my mind. We had our first customer! Even better, we had our first paying customer! This is the break we had been waiting for.

I called Mausmi and told her about the win. We laughed and it felt just great. Then I texted the story of the win to the ThreadSol WhatsApp group. A long-drawn celebration followed on the group with everyone weighing in. Emojis filled up the whole chat space – thumbs-ups, beer mugs, three-finger rock sign, fist pumps . . .

There would be no early morning message reading 27! There would be a message from the bank though – telling us that Rajiv had kept his word and we had our first customer money in our bank account!

This win was an important morale booster for all of us. Secretly all of us wished to see our product score a win before the VC money came in. Two years later, on a sunny December afternoon in Goa, Abhishek confessed to me that if we had raised money first and signed up a customer later, he would have been disappointed. I had had the same wager in my head too. So this was a big victory for us – a big victory for the vision of the product we had created and a vindication of the algorithms and mathematics we had meticulously crafted.

Just a week from the first win, Mausmi closed another deal in Noida with an Adidas factory.

We had trialed at the factory for over six months, and the guys in the factory finally agreed to pay us another $14,000 (₹8 lakh). This was terrific!

In my book, these two were the biggest victories of our start-up journey.

One thing I forgot though – there is always a price to pay!

10

There Is Always a Price to Pay

A few days after our first win, I took the flight back to New Delhi. We, the four founders, had to meet to discuss the cap table. The cap table basically defines who has how much shareholding in the company. It was already decided that we would be raising around $150,000 (₹1 crore) from Blume and the angels, and they would own 20 per cent of ThreadSol. So, ThreadSol's valuation was $750,000 (₹5 crore). We now had to decide the shareholding among us.

By now, it was quite clear how we would shoulder the responsibilities of the business.

It looked like investor relations would be my area. I was also going to be looking at the sales and marketing of ThreadSol. In simple terms, I would have the most external-facing responsibilities of the business. This made me a logical choice to be the CEO of ThreadSol. And as we were a tech start-up, I was also expected to roll up my sleeve and write the algorithms that deliver the fabric savings for IntelloCut, the flagship product of ThreadSol. I used to say the CEO of a start-up is basically a Chief Everything Officer!

Mausmi was taking up the deeper productizing role owing to her industry experience.

Sea, sand and a full moon date…
Lovers? Founders? Soulmates?

She would also lead our software project implementations, customer success and the internal operations of the business. It was clear that she also had the best hand at finance among all of us, so it was decided that finance would be her area. She would be doing front-facing roles in the industry and start-up community events. Mausmi was, thus, given the role of COO (Chief Operating Officer) of ThreadSol.

Abhishek and Bratish were more tech-focused. They took up deep development roles and they were expected to lead product delivery. This would be a critical role for us to deliver and build quality software for our customers. Deep down, we were a tech-driven start-up, and having two people dedicated to technology made a lot of sense. They were to become the tech leaders of ThreadSol. Since we couldn't have two CTOs, they chose to be called the vice-presidents of engineering. Abhishek and Bratish also rolled up their sleeves to help with finance and administration so that we could function smoothly.

Frankly, nobody cared what title each one got. We frequently sought each other's opinions, the opinion of the team members who had the expertise in that particular area.

Often I would go back to my friends to discuss investment options and the sales processes, and they would consult me for their areas. This was all good. But the final hurdle to deriving shareholding numbers proved to be a bit tricky. We set out that afternoon to solve this conundrum over dozens of cups of tea.

The problem was that there was no hard and fast formula to scientifically determine the value of each person in a start-up and therefore to arrive at what should be the derivative shareholding. This is why equity split was a thorny issue among founders. We finally did arrive at a process.

We listed the most important business imperatives. Then, we gave each imperative a relative weight. And finally, we assigned values to what each person brought to the table for each imperative. This gave us a numerical value of what each of us would be contributing to the business's success, which we would use to determine each of our shareholdings in the business.

Let me try to explain this with a quick example.

Say A and B create a start-up and they try to determine the shareholding pattern for themselves. Let's say, they decide that their start-up's biggest business imperatives are: Investment, Sales, Technology, Marketing, Finance, Operations and Administration.

As you can see, the choice of the business imperatives is based on how A and B collectively 'feel' about what needs to exist in their business for it to become successful.

So, let's now draw a grid with these and assign weights on a scale of 5, to each of these imperatives based on the collective experience.

Imperative	*Investment*	*Sales*	*Technology*	*Marketing*	*Finance*	*Operations*	*Administration*
Weight	5	4	4	3	3	2	1

As you can see, the weights are assigned based on how A and B collectively 'feel' about the relative importance of specific business imperatives, and it could be completely different for different businesses.

Now, let's put person A into the grid and estimate what areas A will contribute on a scale of 5 (see table on the facing page).

This way, you estimate the weighted contributions of each team member across all the business imperatives and define their value in the business as one final numerical score.

So, let's say, after doing this we get A's total score = 75 and B's total score = 60. Then, A should own 75/(75+60) = 55.5 per cent and B should own 60/(75+60) = 45.5 per cent.

Imperative	*Investment*	*Sales*	*Technology*	*Marketing*	*Finance*	*Operations*	*Administration*
Weight	5	4	4	3	3	2	1
A's contribution	5	5	3	4	1	1	1
A's Weighted contribution	5*5 = 25	4*5=20	4*3=12	3*4=12	3*1=3	2*1=2	1*1=1
A's Total Weighted Contribution (add all weighted contributions: 25 + 20 + 12 + 12 + 3 + 2 + 1)							75

Now, this is not an exact science. As we discussed this and put the imperatives, their weights and our contribution scores, the discussion became difficult. There were disagreements, emotions, anxieties and insecurities that were laid bare.

Abhishek and I had a row about the assignment of weight for technology imperative in our business. I felt Abhishek was overstating the importance of tech over other imperatives and he thought the other way around. The disagreements grew wider and then finally Mausmi broke the meeting off. Bratish was mostly silent. Mausmi and Bratish were obviously the calm ones. This scene would repeat itself many times in the next five years or so, whenever the four of us met to decide upon the organization's direction, the product's roadmap, terms of investment, etc.

Every time Abhishek and I had a duel, either Mausmi or Bratish, playing the referee, would break our bouts. We would then both walk away from each other and take some time off. Within a few minutes of what would seem like an ugly impasse, Abhishek would always come up with something so funny that we would all laugh and roll on the floor and the tension would lift. Abhishek had this uncanny ability to introduce and dissipate tension at will.

Bratish and Mausmi are deep thinkers and analysers and they simply keep their emotional personalities in check, laying bare their souls on rare occasions. On such occasions, their display would give them rich dividends.

My style of dealing with conflict has always been straightforward and that has worked really well in my co-founders' group. Dealing with conflict is common in a start-up and I think we have a terrific chemistry among the four of us that makes the hardest and the most acrimonious conversations look dead easy and safe.

So, after a whole afternoon of tea, fights and laughs and a bit of Excel sheet work, we had our shareholding. It was decided that I would have 37 per cent ownership, followed by 35 per cent for

Mausmi, 16 per cent for Abhishek and 12 per cent for Bratish. It was no work of Michelangelo, but it was impressive enough for its logical rigour and it achieved the end result splendidly. That evening, we went to a nearby restaurant and celebrated and made some crucial decisions.

We decided that Mausmi and I would move to Bangalore and find a place to stay. We would have our sales, marketing and project-implementation team members come and join us. Abhishek would run the tech team from our current home in Noida. Bratish would hire some of his known tech superstars in Kolkata.

After dinner, as the four of us were chilling at my place, Mausmi's phone rang.

'Guys, our bank account is credited with ₹1 crore ($150,000),' she said. We all high-fived. We had two paying customers and the VC money in our bank. We had a great product. We had a few young and energetic guys who were raring to go.

The story was unfolding and unfolding great for us.

Pondicherry, December 2013

The Dune Eco Resort is a few miles away from the bustling Pondicherry city, and Mausmi and I were staying in a lovely eco-hut right at the beach. Mausmi had planned the outing and booked all the tickets, stay, etc. It was a spectacular property spread across 35 acres right on the Coromandel Coast.

It was a perfect hideaway for both of us to relax, chill out, read our books, take long walks by the pristine beach, feast on the fresh seafood and gulp the freshly brewed beer on the tap.

The resort was almost full, being the end of the holiday season.

However, the place was so enormous that we seldom saw anyone else except in the pool and the restaurant area.

It was a fitting finale to a breathless year where we won the award for being one of India's best start-ups in the Microsoft BizSpark start-up challenge, got many factory trials done in India and abroad, got ourselves a seed round investment from a VC fund and built a team that was young and passionate. It seemed we were finally arriving. And now, here we were, in the lap of nature, for five days of bliss. 2013 was ending in style!

On the penultimate day of our stay, we had some lovely Kerala food. After dinner, Mausmi proposed we go for a stroll at the beach. I agreed.

Let's switch to Mausmi's narrative from here for a better feel of what came next . . .

It was funny to see Manasij at the dinner table. He was on a mission to eat all of Kerala's dishes in one night and he just didn't bother about any rice or bread. It was one long procession of protein cooked in coconut oil.

After dinner, I asked him if he was game for a stroll on the beach. He agreed. We walked on the dirt path from the restaurant to the beachside. The path had lanterns dotted all the way to the sea and soon we reached the beachfront. We walked aimlessly and chatted about this and that. Manasij was talking about the next season of Formula 1 (F1). Frankly, I didn't care about F1. But I knew that Manasij was relaxed as he was talking about something other than the start-up – a good sign.

But I was feeling tense. For the last three days, I was gathering the courage to talk to Manasij. The first two days we both just caught up on sleep and relaxed. Tonight was our last night here. I had to tell him today.

We sat down by the beach. It was a dark, new-moon night, the sea was calm, the winds were gentle. I rested my head on his shoulder. We were silent and at peace – this was the right moment.

'Manasij, I have something to tell you. You cannot freak out,' I said.

He immediately sat up.

'I am pregnant.'

'What? How? I mean . . .' He was searching for words. I was sure he was freaked out.

'What are we going to do? This is . . .' He was still searching for words.

Then he got up and began pacing.

'I mean, how are we going to handle this? No, no, no, no . . . this was not what we planned . . .'

I cannot say I was not freaked out. But I had had time to reflect on this and was prepared. For Manasij, it was a shock. I have to admit a part of me was amused by his neurotic state. He seemed to have lost the ability to form a complete sentence. It was funny.

We had been married for nine years and we didn't want kids. It's not as if we didn't like kids – we did – but we just didn't want them for us. That had been our joint decision. And here we were . . .

After a while, he calmed down and finally found the right question.

'What do you want to do about it?' he asked.

We spoke for hours together sitting by the waves on the beach. As the night progressed, the waves came in deeper with the rising tides. We laughed and cried, retreating further back as the sea came in. We kissed and held hands. The sea bore witness to one of the deepest conversations we had had. On that dark night, sitting by the sea, our bond grew even deeper.

Now, back to me.

When we walked back to our hut that night, I was at peace. I didn't want Mausmi to compromise on her life. She had just helped us create something that the world had not seen before. It would be unfair to not let her play a big part in this journey. Time and time again, women have made these sacrifices. Have those sacrifices rewarded women equally?

The choice was cut out: do we go ahead and try and build ourselves a life that we had dreamt of or embrace the biological eventuality? We chose the former. Sometimes, life presents these binaries, and the choices we make define who we are and how satisfied and content we will be later in our lives.

But the decision was incredibly emotional and difficult. I hadn't expected it to be so hard. We have never spoken about this to anyone – until now. Entrepreneurship is a battle with yourself. And most of the scars you bear are private. You don't make an exhibition of yourself. You take the blows and writhe in pain – but you do that silently. Externally, you project supreme confidence and unabashed coolness. This makes many believe that entrepreneurship is not a difficult path and if they worked a little bit at it, it will be within their grasp.

Well, the reality is quite far away from this. The most common anxieties and problems with becoming an entrepreneur are pretty well documented and understood. Where will you find co-founders or raise money from, or how will you get the first customers or enthuse people to join you? These are known. But the real problems are very different.

Where will you find co-founders is not the real problem. The real problem is – will you have enough humility to accept some other guy as your equal and have the ability to disagree and yet not disrespect them, fight, yet not fall out.

Where will you raise money from or how will you get the first customers is not the real problem. The real problem is – will you have the self-belief to be rejected time and time and time again and yet, not allow that vulnerability to break your fortitude, self-belief and self-worth.

How will you enthuse people to join you is not the real problem. The real problem is – will you have enough gas in the tank that despite all the madness and rejections and negativity around you still have the stature to lift someone else and inspire them.

These are battles with the self. Most people don't become entrepreneurs not because they didn't have that great idea or they could not find the seed round cheque but because they just do not have the stomach to go to battle with themselves for a sustained period.

And as every battle demands, there are costs involved. There is always a price to pay. And if you are not ready to pay the price, there is no admission ticket for you on this ride. And entrepreneurship will ask for that pound of flesh when you least expect it.

As 2013 drew to a close, my transition from a rookie to an entrepreneur was complete. I was still not a hard-nosed entrepreneur – but I was getting better at being one.

If I close my eyes, I can still hear the waves crashing at our feet on that dark starlit night at the beach in Pondicherry and I hear Mausmi's voice in my ears – 'This is a start of a new chapter. Let's grow this!'

Part II

Let's Grow This . . .

Let's go international . . .

Let's build a team . . .

Let's grow and grow . . .

Narayana Murthy invests in us . . .

Are we going to die again?

Riots, killings, arson – conditions are dire
You press on – it is trial by fire…

11

Trial by Fire

The alarm was loud. 3.45 a.m. *Aargghhhh!*

I sat up on the bed and wished I could go back to sleep. And then as the alarm screamed again at 4 a.m., I leapt into the shower. I had to be ready in 30 minutes. No more time to sulk.

I came to the hotel reception at 4.30 a.m. dressed sharply in my black suit and tie. I was greeted by a young man in his early twenties. He was my ride. He asked me to follow him to the porch. I walked through the hotel's revolving doors into the porch and saw a big green ambulance standing.

'Wow, somebody is sick in the hotel,' I thought.

To my utter surprise, the young man opened the ambulance door and asked me to hop in.

I looked at the guy in shock and then said to him in my fluent Bengali, 'Are you sure, I have to travel in an ambulance?'

The young man was equally shocked to hear me speak in Bengali.

'Sir, this is the only safe mode of transport right now. There are riots in the city and they are burning public property and private cars. They let the ambulances go. This is the safest way to travel. Don't worry, we will reach safely.'

Then he took a pause and said, 'If we see trouble, I will make a detour and if we get caught, please don't talk to them in Bengali. Speak in English. They will let you go.'

'And what about you?' I asked.

He looked at me for a few seconds as if he was searching for the right response and said, 'You will be fine.'

I was in Chittagong, Bangladesh. It was early 2015 and the country had been torn apart by political violence between two rival political parties. Petrol bombing cars and properties were the most popular weapon for rioters, and the country was ravaged by these attacks. In fact, you could casually stroll on the roads and buy petrol bombs for ₹100 ($1.5). These were glass bottles of Coca-Cola that were full of petrol and a makeshift cloth wick was placed on each bottle to light it. Once you light it, you throw it at your enemy. The bottle shatters, and the petrol ignites with a frightening blast and burns down the thing it lands on.

I had just entered the country to close a $250,000 deal with one of the largest denim manufacturers of Bangladesh. This was my first trip to the country. As a Bengali, I had heard about Bangladesh often while I was growing up. My mother's side had come from downtown Dhaka, migrating to India in 1947. My grandparents used to speak about Bangladesh as if it was some promised land.

Apparently, when they left Dhaka in a hurry to escape the communal violence, they didn't dispose of the land and the property they owned. My great-grandfather had founded one of the biggest boys' schools in Dhaka. At home, any discussion about Bangladesh would always be very emotional, veering between joy and tears and guilt. My parents dreamt of visiting Bangladesh. As I was flying into Dhaka, my mind was full of these thoughts.

Dhaka's areal approach gives you a glimpse of a typical low-income nation. There is an unbelievable density of low-rise buildings that strangely have no paint coatings. So, you see a large swathe of naked brick structures and narrow clogged roads running between them. The airstrip was surrounded by marshes. It was old and looked nothing like the modern glass and steel buildings that you see in most contemporary airport designs.

What the ambulance driver had told me was echoed everywhere. I was told that except for an absolute emergency, I should never speak in Bengali as I would stop getting the preferred foreigner treatment. It is strange. But anyone who is born and brought up in the Indian subcontinent knows this drill. You need to sound elite, more fancy, richer and better educated to be treated better.

Getting better treatment for being an elite exists everywhere in the world. But the Indian subcontinent overdoes it because of the sheer population load of the commoners, which makes being one of the many disadvantageous by a large margin. You can never replicate this anywhere in the world. Everywhere else, being one with the commons is helpful. Not here.

In Dhaka airport, I could hear and understand everything that was being said around me. I could read all the instructions, signs, etc. but I maintained a studied detachment. I spoke only English and tried to look as foreign and posh as possible. My long hair and dark shades added to my exotic looks. Result? I sailed through immigration and customs in seconds.

I was exchanging WhatsApp messages with Anas (we had hired him for helping me with sales, remember?), who was living in Dhaka at the time and was due to meet me for a short catch-up before I took my next flight to Chittagong. As I came out, I stopped and lit a cigarette, and for the first time, put my phone down and looked up. I was hit by a sight that I cannot forget even today.

I was standing on a large arrival porch where cars would come and pick up passengers. It was around 200 feet long, and there were 50 feet high iron grills running the entire length.

On the other side of the tall iron grills, there were thousands of people, standing with their faces glued to the iron grill, watching you. Their clothes were dirty and torn, and they were standing there, saying nothing, just watching rich people. Thousands of eyes were on me. They saw this rich guy coming from an exotic foreign land, with long hair and dark shades, wearing sporty shorts and a sleeveless tee that exposed his tattoos, with a cigarette in one hand and an expensive mobile in another.

I froze. The scene creeped the hell out of me. I have seen enough poverty and despair in India. But in India, when I would look at poverty, it would be the specimen. Here, it was the opposite. The rich were the specimen. The poor and despairing come to the airport to watch the rich. This was their escape from the oppressing grind of their lives. It was hard to ignore this terrible fact. It hit me like a punch in my gut. I felt nauseated.

That evening I landed in Chittagong, I had to wait until midnight for the factory to arrange a pick-up for me from the airport to the hotel when everyone hoped it was safer to travel. I had reached the hotel almost at 1 a.m., and I was ready to go again at 4.30 a.m. in an ambulance.

As the ambulance started from my hotel, I could see burnt remains of cars on the street, still smoldering. The roadside shops and establishments showed signs of violence. The streets were deserted, and the ambulance tore through the empty roads and galloped into the factory in less than 15 minutes. On a normal day, it would have been an hour's drive through the chaotic and ramshackle roads.

My meeting at the factory went well. The management was there at 5 a.m. and we finished the deal-making in less than 30 minutes. Yes, we had the $250,000 deal in the hand for five factories at $50,000 per factory! It was decided that the moment the situation improved, we would be able to implement the project.

Apparently, these guys did not close deals unless the bosses met the owner of the company they were going to deal with, especially when the deal was worth so much money!

The drive back to the airport was tense. The first light of the day was breaking, and the deserted city looked more terrifying. At a crossroads, the police stopped the ambulance. There was some fresh disturbance and we could see flames at a distance. The ambulance took a detour. The young driver and I both were silent, and I could feel the palpable tension in the air.

As I reached the airport and thanked the young guy for his help, he turned and said, 'I never expected anyone from out of Bangladesh to come to us now. But you and your company people keep coming. This place is burning, yet you guys come.' I guess that's the closest to a salute one can get in civilian life.

As I made my way to the check-in counter, I could not help but reflect on the last 12 hours. I had seen poverty, violence and finally got a win for us. Bangladesh was the second biggest manufacturing destination in the world after China. Getting a win here was critical for us. This was the first large Bangladesh factory group that had closed the deal with us. It was a big occasion.

As the plane took off, I could see dark black smoke rising from parts of the city.

Wow, the trial by fire was over.

Well, not quite. Our team came three weeks later, in February 2015, to implement the software at Chittagong and they did their work in a similar environment – travelling every day in ambulances and yet not giving up despite all the odds. The fire within to succeed was burning brighter than the fires around us.

Where did this come from? If I could retrace our paths, it started in Sri Lanka.

Let's recount Lanka Dahan for you . . .

12

Lanka Dahan

Why is Ecuador important in the story of evolution? This simple question might stump many people. In 1853, Charles Darwin visited the Galapagos Islands, a province of Ecuador in the Pacific Ocean where he spent many months understanding the unique flora and fauna and came to realize his brilliant theory.

Galapagos is 1,000 kilometres off the coast of Ecuador. The high seas had kept this island completely separated from the mainland and thus for millions of years the animals and the vegetation had an undisturbed opportunity to evolve, adapt and become unique. Today, we know of many such island-Edens – Socotra islands off Yemen, Madagascar Islands off southeast Africa, the whole of New Zealand's North and South Islands and so on. All these islands were cut off from the mainland and developed surprising lifeforms that are very different from the mainland's ecospheres.

The lesson is slightly tangential I admit. Islands are important. And, it was for our story as well. Sri Lanka became the place where ThreadSol's story took some serious flight and grew into something worthy of a book one day.

It began with a phone call that came while Mausmi and I were driving back from Pondicherry at the end of 2013. We had stopped for a tea break along the highway near Salem, and I got a call on my mobile from an international number. It was unusual to get a foreign number call on my mobile back then.

'Is this Een-tay-law-CUT?' Someone with a very thick Sri Lankan accent was on the line.

A quick thing about the Sri Lankan accent – it sounds very close to a Tamil-Malayalam mix but with an added stress at the end syllable. So, cricket is pronounced as 'Kree-CUT', wicket 'Wee-CUT' and so on. Years of listening to Sri Lankan cricket commentators had tuned my ears to the tones and enunciations of the accent, so I had no problem understanding it.

'Yes, this is Een-tay-law-CUT,' I said.

'I am calling from Sri Lanka. We produce denim. Can you come and show us your software?'

This was surprising, no one had ever called us from abroad for a demo, and here was someone from Sri Lanka calling me.

'How did you know about us?' I asked.

'You have a website, don't you?' Pat came the reply.

'Wow.' I was impressed. Never had any Indian manufacturer ever mentioned our website and at that time our search scores were so low that unless you were a psychopathic killer or a lone-wolf FBI agent, the chances were that you could never find our website. And here was someone who had not just found it but also taken the pain to call and, that too, all the way from Sri Lanka!

So, in January 2014, when I was flying to Sri Lanka, I had an inkling that our island neighbour might be different from India, just like Galapagos was different from the mainland. How different was Sri Lanka? I was about to find out.

My start on the island was, however, less than auspicious. I landed early evening, and since my meeting was the next morning, I ventured out to the streets and ate local food. I had heard a lot of stories about how amazing the Sri Lankan string hopper was, and I wanted to give it a try. It is basically a distant cousin of the dosa and appam. It was not amazing and it didn't blow my mind.

I was staying in a cheap area of Colombo known as Wellawatta, a predominantly residential area for the Tamil community. The hotel had a fancy name, Green Palace Inn, but it was basically a giant shoe box whose first three floors were cheap banquet halls where lower-middle-income families held their wedding functions. The fourth and fifth floors were mostly reserved for the wedding party guests, who were always super noisy.

There was no room service and they only changed the linen when you checked out or probably died in the hotel room. If you wanted to get clean sheets, you had to carry the linen to a nearby washing machine parlour and pay to get them washed and then bring them back to your room. The room was just a little bigger than a family car and had no windows.

Whosoever designed the hotel must have been a real maverick. The corridors had bright red el-cheapo plastic matting. The room walls were painted in fluorescent green that could damage your cornea if you gazed at it long enough without Mylar shades. The bathrooms had blue-and-white chessboard tiles.

The whole place was a cornucopia of colours, all at war with the other. There were, however, two great things about the hotel – one, it had blazing-fast WiFi and two, the air-conditioning worked like a charm; and for $30 a night, it was a terrific bargain. I came back to Green Palace Inn many times and stayed there for a month each time in that windowless colourful riot of a room where I would have the same food for dinner for each of the 30 nights of my stay – a McChicken burger with fries and coke!

And the reason for such a sad dinner routine was because of my first night in Colombo.

The Sri Lankan string hopper staged a serious international food conflict in my stomach. By midnight, I was running a high fever and had radiating pain in my stomach and tingling all over my body. I was sick for more than two hours. By then, I had already consumed a lot of water and forced my stomach contents out by sticking my fingers down my throat. Still, the fever, pain and tingling didn't subside.

At 1 a.m., I took an Uber and went to the emergency room of a nearby hospital. The doctors and the attendants were very gracious and helpful. They did a few tests and hooked me to an IV drip. As the pain subsided, I drifted off to a peaceful sleep in the hospital emergency room.

By 5.30 a.m., I was feeling as fit and fierce as a gazelle. I asked the doctors to let me go, but to my immense surprise they didn't agree. They wanted to monitor me for a day. I couldn't afford that. My meeting was at 10 a.m. and there was no way I was going to miss that. So, after a bit of haggling, they let me go AMA (against medical advice).

I reached the hotel at 6.30 a.m., showered and shaved, got dressed in my jacket and tie and took the cab for a three-hour car ride to Avissawella, 100 kilometres from Colombo. The road was long and continuously twisty all along. Later, I found out that all Sri Lankan roads were like that – endless dual carriageway twisties with no grade separators anywhere flanked by lush greenery, paddy fields and ponds.

The factory was enormous. It had a huge manicured lawn with fancy bright green Korean grass that the people in Sri Lanka just love. On the side of the lawn stood the neatly parked fleet of cars that the people in Sri Lanka just love. The reception was three stories tall. It was a glass and granite construction, which the people in Sri Lanka just love. The whole architecture was a modern art deco, which the people in Sri Lanka just love. The whole factory was air-conditioned and spotlessly clean, which the people in Sri Lanka just love. The factory was filled with men who were all wearing trousers made of shiny fabric and had tight body-fit shirts with black pointy shoes, which the people in Sri Lanka just love. The women were dressed in skirts and blouses, which the people in Sri Lanka just love. I loved all of these instantly.

It was such a big departure from the dirty and grimy factories that I had seen in India. This looked like a lovely corporate bank or a glittering software company that you see in downtown Bangalore or Mumbai. Every floor was air-conditioned, a huge leap from India's hot and humid factory floors. In front of the Sri Lankan factories, the Indian factories almost look like large tailoring shops. I was impressed with the setup immediately.

Factories have always fascinated me. I grew up in Patna, where there were no nearby large factories. My earliest recollection of seeing any factory came from my childhood train journeys to Kolkata. There were some mega coal-refining factories at the border of Bihar and Bengal. The overnight train from Patna would cross this belt dead in the night and I recall seeing the fire-breathing, smoke-belching, metal- and conveyer-belt-infested behemoths as we snaked by.

They looked like living-breathing-moving monsters that consumed coal and had a fire in their guts with tall chimneys that looked like giants' legs. As the train would pull away, I would keep my nose firmly pressed on the window's iron grills – looking at the ever-diminishing monster until it had become a tiny speck of light.

This Sri Lankan factory reminded me of that childhood experience. The only difference was that I was inside the monster's gut.

As I set up my laptop for the demo, almost 20 people poured into the conference room. I had not seen so many people come for a software demo in any Indian factory before. The CEO, the COO, the CFO – everyone was there. The demo went on for two hours. It was clear that the CEO, Lalith, was the kingpin and the most intelligent fella in the room. He spoke with an American accent and was quick to grasp the details of the product. He asked almost all the questions and explained to his fellowmen what the solution could do for them. At the end of the meeting, he invited me for a discussion in his private chambers.

'Look Manasij, we would like to buy your software,' Lalith opened the discussions with this line.

I was delighted. It seemed like the best result that I could get on my first trip to Sri Lanka.

'We buy $10 million fabric every year. If we save just 1 per cent, we will save $100,000 fabric every year. I am interested in doing this,' Lalith continued. 'What is the price of the software?'

I was not fully prepared to answer this question.

We had sold IntelloCut to a few factories in India, and the best price we got there was $15,000.

What should I say?

$20,000?

$25,000?

'$32,000,' I said.

'And two of our consultants will come to implement; you will pay for their return airfare and their hotel accommodation with all meals.'

I put all my cards on the table and braced for impact.

Lalit looked at me and extended his right hand. 'You have a deal, my friend. Now, let's eat. You must be hungry.'

I shook his hand but declined the lunch offer. I was fresh from my food poisoning debacle and didn't want to risk having Sri Lankan food again.

And that was that. The first time I came to Sri Lanka, I was able to sell the software for twice the price that I was able to garner in India. The discussion was always reasonable, and the factory looked spic-and-span. This is how different the island nation of

Sri Lanka looked to me from mainland India. Sri Lanka was the Galapagos for us.

Four years later, I met Lalit again in a lovely colonial cricket club bar in Colombo. Lalit had moved on from apparel manufacturing and was the CEO of Sri Lankan Airlines for a while and then settled into the role of the CEO of the Sri Lankan tea giant Dilmah.

We shared a hearty laugh when I told him that I had sold the solution to him for twice the price of what we used to, and Lalit surprised me by saying that he had been willing to pay $50,000 that afternoon and I had indeed offered him a sweet deal. Everyone on the deal table had been a winner that day in early January 2014.

I returned from Colombo victorious. Just like Lord Hanuman. This was our moment of the mythical Lanka Dahan (Sri Lanka on fire). This was our first international deal and at a handsome price point. And from here on, we realized, ThreadSol's business lay in international markets and it's where we pivoted. In the following years, our clients would come from Bangladesh to Vietnam to China and, of course, Sri Lanka – but we never had a substantial client base in India.

It was a sunny January morning when I returned to Bangalore, our new home. As I was making my way from the airport to home, my phone rang.

'Hey, this is Velu. Remember me?'

It was Velu, the guy who had said he would help us raise capital and I had agreed to share 5 per cent of the raised capital if he helped close an investment deal.

'Yes, I do remember. Hey Velu, how are you doing?' I said.

'Listen, I saw that you raised the seed round. Good going. Now when are you paying me?'

I was puzzled. Velu had had no role in the fundraising. I didn't understand why he was asking for money.

'Why do you think we owe you any money, Velu?' I asked.

'I talked you up to your investors. Without me doing that, Blume never would have invested.' Velu was purely scamming me here.

'Look, Velu, I don't think you had any role to play. So, sorry I am not paying you anything here.'

I was polite but firm.

He haggled on for a few more minutes. Soon the discussion became hostile and vitriolic.

'You think you are some smart dude here, don't you? Mark my words, if you cross me, I will personally ensure that you can never raise a penny from any investor in India.' He was hissing now. And then he disconnected the call abruptly.

I looked at my phone in disbelief. I had heard that there are all kinds of characters in the Indian start-up ecosystem. But this rattled me. I was nervous and unsure for a moment.

Could he actually hurt us?

Did I make a mistake by picking up a bone with Velu?

What if he could do what he said?

Moments later, I forgot all about him. The victory in Sri Lanka and the $32,000 price tag for our software was such a terrific kick that I was again back to feeling good.

But this was not the last I would hear from Velu. I had no idea that he and I were headed for another showdown. And where would that happen?

New Delhi?

Bangalore?

Mumbai?

Nope . . .

Sri Lanka – of all the places in the world!

The Island

Vol. 34 No.89 Wednesday 9th July 2014. 11 pages Rs.25 Registered in Sri Lanka as a Newspaper

NOTICE

Ve regret to inform ur readers that one f our main factories ave been suspended or a day due to estoration.

ThreadSol wins 1st the Venture Engine startup show

14 (day/night). Sri Toss: Sri Lanka. re, free-scoring best, re hundred was not series. It was the first rnational hundreds African victory. In the ed Sri Lankan attack, e patience to spend npany; the rest folded nbitious and e strokes. Dilshan t, enjoying fortune ed the second ball of his bowling hand with hove him from the did later re-emerge ur). Dilshan was on ired in 11 one-day t Pallekele until he off his glove. On a Lanka subsided, e costly. Nor did the on a DRS-related ir won an lbw eeping Jayawardene, urned it on review he ball had sped oundary but, as nically been out at not stand.

July 9th Colombo: ThreadSol won the 1st Venture Engine startup show at Kingsbury hotel last evening. Venture Engine is Sri Lanka's most prominent startup award show. Over 100 startups from 4 countries applied for Venture Engine. The Top 10 startups were choser for a shootout and ThreadSol came on top. The event was attended by over 300 people and over 50 investors from Sri

We win Sri Lanka . . . Colombo to Galle

Three cheers for ThreadSol . . .

13

Sri Lanka – Of All the Places in the World!

If you haven't seen *Erin Brockovich*, you should.

I like the scene where PG&E, a global corporate giant, sends a fleet of their lawyers to Ed Masry's (played by the lovable Albert Finny) small law firm. Five menacing looking, sharply dressed lawyers representing PG&E swoop in to browbeat Ed Masry and Erin Brockovich into accepting a lowballed settlement. The streetfighter Ed Masry recognizes the scare tactics and responds in a comically theatric display of counter-intimidation. He asks his secretary, the typist and a low functionary of his office, all with no legal experience, to join him and Erin in the conference room with a pile of files to pay the vultures in the same coin – scare them back with numerical mass and a pile of paper.

Long story short – they win.

I like that scene for its comic value as well as for the depiction of the scare tactics from both sides. Sometimes you need solid theatrics to pull off something that arguments and numbers will not achieve.

On a rainy afternoon in April 2014, this scene was replayed in the board room of one of Sri Lanka's biggest manufacturing groups where we were trialing our software. At that time, Sri Lanka had shown the potential of becoming a serious cash cow for us and it was important that we won some big deals there. Unlike India, where apparel manufacturing has stagnated into a small- and medium-scale enterprise and remained rooted in deep archaic systems resistant to change and more resistant to pay for software, Sri Lanka had embraced technology as its lynchpin.

For all apparel tech products, Sri Lanka was a veritable Mecca. We were seeing the signs of this and therefore through 2014 we focused really hard on this small island Eden garden for our business. And we landed our biggest break in Sri Lanka with MAS Holdings – a billion-dollar-sized manufacturing group that is the official sponsor of the Sri Lanka cricket team even today.

Mausmi, Jaya, Anas and I were conducting a two-week trial in this lovely MAS Holdings' sportswear factory 100 kilometres from Colombo after I had given their group director a two-hour presentation explaining what our software could do for them. The guy was not fully convinced with my presentation but was intrigued enough to offer us a two-week trial in their 'best factory in the group'. If we could show them fabric savings, we could get 40 factories in their group to buy our software. That would be a $2-million-dollar deal! But first, we had to win the two-week trial.

Almost immediately, we realized that we were facing a hostile management. The factory management was told by the group director that some smart Indian kids were coming to show them their flaws and trial a software to show how to rectify them. Obviously, the factory management, who were the proud tag-bearers of the 'best factory in the group', didn't take this kindly and the internal communication gaffe fell on our heads like ten tons of harassment, non-cooperation and sabotage.

On the first day, we were made to wait for six hours in a room that felt like being in the Kalahari Desert as the AC was purposely kept in non-cooling mode. Second, we were assigned a shift from 5 a.m. to 1 p.m. In a day or two, we found out that we could never leave at 1 p.m. as most of our work would need interfacing with people who would purposely give us meeting times after 1 p.m. So, our work time became 5 a.m. to 8 p.m. every day, six days a week. Third, we would have to endlessly wait for people to arrive for meetings and they would always cancel. The first week was a complete washout and we could not get anything done in the factory.

In the second week, we arrested the slide. By sheer will and tenacity, we managed to stem the onslaught and posted big results on the floor with our software. Every time we showed the results to the management, they sneered and dismissed them as fluke. It was extremely humiliating.

We knew we would get our chance when the group director would come in for the two-week review. We knew we could show him the results. They also knew this. And once they saw we could pose positive results, all hell broke loose. They put all their people to beat our software plans. They would see the results from our software and then press their folks to try multiple combinations to find better plans manually. They failed. But this exacted a terrible cost on both parties. Both sides worked long hours to beat each other.

In the meantime, the day of the final evaluation by the group director drew in. The night before the big meeting, it rained so hard that all our rooms got waterlogged. We were all without rooms until about 2 a.m. and spent most of the night in the reception battling mosquitoes.

'How are we going to win against these guys?' Anas wondered. He was a 22-year-old kid straight out of college and was equally amused and aghast seeing the open hostility.

'We need to put up a show. These guys are going to come after us big time tomorrow,' Mausmi said. 'We need to have a plan to tackle this. We have results, but we need more.'

'What show can we put up?' Jaya asked. She was handling the floor and was positively exasperated. So, we brainstormed and came up with a plan.

The next day, the meeting was at 3 p.m. in the board room. The room had an oval table and at the end of the table was a large projector.

The group director arrived. He sat at the end of the table facing the big projector. There were seven people from the factory; all came and sat around the table. Then Jaya walked in with two assistants who had carried some 40 files with them. They walked in full view of the sitting group and neatly stacked the 40 files on the table. Then Anas and I walked in with all our laptops and a printer and set it up in the middle of the table. Finally, Mausmi walked in with two assistants who had carried all the saved fabric and placed that on the table. Props were in place – it was go-time.

'We are ready to show you how we studied all your orders that are in these files,' Mausmi started with an assuring calm voice and pointed at the large pile of files.

'And we will print for you all the reports right here from the software with this printer.' And then she took a dramatic pause.

'We will then show you how we saved you this amount of fabric for your business,' she showed the saved fabric in the middle of the table.

'Shall we begin and see how we saved you 3 per cent fabric?' she asked.

The room was silent, and the group director nodded.

Two hours later, four of us were sitting in our hotel bar with chilled bottles of Sri Lankan Lion beer in our hands. We had won. We were laughing and giggling like school kids. The show had been a hit. The theatrics of walking with files and printers and saved fabric with assistants had worked. We had our foot in the door of the largest Sri Lankan group and we could get their 40 factories. Erin Brockovich and Ed Masry had won against PG&E. Again!

If you win a Test match against the formidable Aussies in Perth, Australia, regarded as the fastest and most unforgiving bouncy pitches in the world, you can say your Test team is awesome. Similarly, if you get MAS in Sri Lanka, you should believe you are one of the very best. When we won at MAS, we had just proven that we truly were world-class. At that time our revenue was around $60,000 and we had just two–three customers. But this win meant that we could now expect to win big internationally.

3 a.m.

It was a warm and humid night in May 2014. The rains had just stopped.

Bratish and I stood on the balcony. I lit a cigarette and we sipped our hot, steaming tea. We were both tense. On the dark cloudy night, we could hear a symphony of mating calls of crickets and frogs. Somehow, in Colombo, you could still hear the insects and frogs – sounds increasingly absent from some Indian cities.

Nature in Sri Lanka was always plentiful and accessible, while in Indian cities, nature is mostly replaced by a central patch of green in every residential society, for which you pay preferential rates per square foot. However, both of us were unmindful of the romance of this dark cloudy night. There was a storm coming for us the next morning.

Finally, Bratish broke the silence. 'What do you reckon our chances are?'

'I don't know Bratish,' I said, 'I really don't know.'

'You know, if you spin the chamber so many times, sometimes you do get a bullet.' Bratish was getting philosophical.

'Maybe we should not have gotten ourselves into this mess,' he finished.

'Yes, maybe,' I said.

The moment we finished our tea, we jumped back into our chairs and began looking at the software code. We had five hours before the car came to fetch us for one of the biggest tests of our start-up. Today would be the day when we will get to know if the sacrifice of four weeks of sleep and round-the-clock coding and product building by a dozen people made any sense or not.

At 9 a.m., Bratish and I were scheduled to run a live test to see if we could reduce the fabric buying of the largest sportswear manufacturer in Sri Lanka. We were up against three competing software solutions – all long-term players from the US, Israel and New Zealand. These guys had been in business for over 15 years. In comparison, our code was still compiling and had bugs and was less than four weeks old.

At 8 a.m. the car came to pick us up. The ride was almost 45 minutes and both of us fell into a deep sleep in the car as it negotiated the heavy traffic of Colombo. We reached the lovely headquarters and set up our systems in the main boardroom. There were six officials from their side and the board room had a lovely spread of sandwiches and tea for us. We had no appetite. We were both tense and sleep-deprived and very nervous.

At 9.30 a.m. we had uploaded 10,000 orders from the last year through a mega Excel sheet. The software was now digesting the 10,000 orders. It took a little over 30 minutes to do so. We had the results and the six executives took the results and went in. They would take a little over five hours to check our results manually and we would know if we won or lost at 3 p.m.

We were free for now. The unbelievable effort of the last four weeks, the sleepless nights, the breathless code writing, testing, bug fixing and deploying had ended, and now the only thing that we could do was wait. And waiting was excruciating. Bratish and I were wiped out. We sat in the adjoining garden, both of us too exhausted to talk.

'I think we will win,' said Bratish.

Then he compensated.

'I think there is a good chance that we will win. What do you think?'

'I don't know. I just hope all this effort means something,' I said.

'I still can't believe we got into this. How did we get into this mess?' Bratish reflected.

It had all started four weeks back just after we had won our *Erin Brockovich*-styled trial in Sri Lanka.

One Sunday, in the middle of April 2014, I got this:

> Dear Manasij,
>
> I found ThreadSol on LinkedIn and thought to reach out to you.
>
> As a business, we process 10,000 orders and we buy over $150 million fabric every year.
>
> Can your tool help us plan fabric buying in bulk and save us some cost?
>
> Regards,
>
> Chandrakumar Theivendran (CK)

I looked at the LinkedIn InMail and pondered. Our product 'IntelloCut' could not do this.

Think about a scenario where you have to throw a party with say 10,000 guests and you have decided on a catering service to cook the food for your party. Before the caterer starts the food preparation, someone has to estimate how much groceries to buy for the caterers. Once the groceries are bought, then the caterer can efficiently plan the use of the raw material to prepare the food.

Similarly, if you are a manufacturer and you win an order to make 10,000 denim trousers for Levi's, you will have to estimate the amount of fabric that would be needed and then buy that fabric. This estimation happens at the headquarters of the manufacturers. After the fabric is bought, you will pass the order and the fabric from the headquarters to one of your factories. In the factory, IntelloCut could plan the fabric use for you and make the 10,000 denim bottoms. However, we had no solution at the headquarters level to take care of the buying optimization problem.

This was what CK was asking us to help him with. We didn't have any solution that could do this. However, it was not a million miles away and we could do this if we had six months.

So, I wrote back to CK and said I would love to get on a call with him tc understand more. We had a long discussion. He mentioned that he had already completed the trials with three software from the US, Israel and New Zealand and was going to decide in the next four weeks. If we had a solution, we should show him in the next four weeks, but we needed to better the results that he had.

'Four weeks, Manasij. Four weeks. After that, it is any one of the three and not you,' CK said. He was an affable and logical guy and the fact that he was willing to give us an opportunity meant a lot to me. No one sticks their neck out in a corporate job and gives start-ups opportunities unless they themselves are visionaries. CK was one of them. He had given us an opportunity and it was up to us to take that and make something out of it.

I decided to go for it. No one had achieved something without risking anything. Let's do it.

I scrambled an all-hands meeting at ThreadSol over Skype. I told the team that the prize was very big. If we could win this, we would add another solution to our portfolio and become an even more well-rounded solution provider. But, if we aspired to do this, we all would have to put up an all-out effort and attempt to do what should take six months in just four weeks. There could be no half measures. There could be no off days. We needed to deliver 24x7 work to build something that could defeat the decade-old incumbents. This was a call for sacrifice and courage.

The whole company responded as if we were under attack. The development team under Bratish and Abhishek went into war mode. Bratish had hired four people in Kolkata and he had rented a small flat that we called our 'Kolkata office'. The guys had put in mattresses and bedsheets and camped out for a 24x7 code-writing spree.

The war cry was 'Write the code, buy AC with remote.'

Abhishek was operating his development team of three from our Noida office, which remained our old two-bed flat. The war cry at the Noida office was 'No deal, no motorcycle' – a reference to our team member, Santosh, wanting to buy a motorcycle.

Our Bangalore home office had nine, including Mausmi and me. We were doing continuous testing 24x7 and reporting bugs and issues. It seemed like an army preparing for an attack.

Now here we were, Bratish and I, sitting in an ante-garden of the board room nervously waiting for the results. Everyone in ThreadSol held their breath. It was the moment of truth.

Bratish and I were called in for a high tea at 3 p.m. with CK in the boardroom. As we walked in, we saw all the executives with CK. They were all smiling. CK extended his hand – 'Congratulations guys, your results have come out to be the best and fastest. We will be saving around $5 million with your solution. By the way, what is the name of your software?'

That was the day of the genesis of our second software product – IntelloBuy! Bratish and I felt a deep sense of relief. We both slept like babies on the way back in the car.

We were too tired to celebrate or go out or paint the town red.

We had another innovation under our belt. IntelloBuy solves the buying problem and buys the right amount of fabric for a business and IntelloCut takes that fabric and plans the most optimized manufacturing for a factory. We were now a well-rounded solution.

That afternoon, Abhishek took Santosh to the nearby bike shop and bought him the bike of his dreams by swiping his credit card.

'No need to take a loan from the bank. You pay me when you have the money.' Abhishek's impulsive warm character was on full display on this red-letter day.

Tripurari and Surajit went and bought an AC for their office in Kolkata. These guys could now work in air-conditioned comfort rather than toiling in Kolkata's heat and humid climate.

Sri Lanka turned into our biggest customer base in 2014. In July, I received a call from our angel investor, Rajan Anandan.

'Hey, Manasij. Have you heard of Venture Engine in Sri Lanka?' Rajan asked.

'No, what is this?' I said.

'Well, it is a start-up award competition that will showcase the best of Sri Lanka start-ups and all the major Sri Lanka investors would be there. All the big apparel business owners in Sri Lanka are big investors and if they like you, you can get more business, and also investment doors could open for you. I think you should do this.' Rajan was as matter-of-fact as he always was, and it was a delight to see him take interest in our progress.

So, we applied. There were a few rounds of screening and we were eventually invited to pitch at the Venture Engine grand finale in the charming Kingsbury Hotel's banquet hall along with nine other start-ups from Sri Lanka.

It was a lavish affair. The banquet was tastefully decorated; and Colombo's elite – a jamboree of well-dressed men and women – were part of the audience. For the founders, these events were super serious. You could see them going over their pitch deck one last time and looking nervously at the watch. The investors and socialites, on the other hand, glided effortlessly around the bar with drinks in hand.

The show started, and the host announced the sequence of the events. Every entrepreneur would get 10 minutes for their pitch and five minutes for the question and answer round. After that, there was a 45-minute fashion show and then the declaration of results.

The host welcomed all the dignitaries and proceeded to introduce the judges for the evening.

There were seven judges and the host introduced six of them. And said, 'And finally, the head of the judging committee, please welcome Mr Velu from Bangalore, India.'

I had no mirror in front of me, but if there was, my reflection would show that I had turned white.

On the stage was the guy, who just a few months back had threatened me that I wouldn't see another cent of investment.

How could this happen?

What happens now?

Is he going to kill me on stage in front of all investors and factory owners?

No, no, no, no . . . This is not happening.

I buried my face in my palms and put my head down. Velu finished speaking. The event began. I was supposed to be the first speaker on stage and my name was announced.

As I got on stage, I looked down at Velu and our eyes locked. I don't know how the fear and anxiety that had washed over me just moments back sublimated into composure but I ended up doing a near-perfect waltz. I moved around the stage and watched the eyes of the audience following me. I raised the pitch of the voice and lowered it to introduce drama; I used pauses to augment the weight of the delivery and used humour and jokes to deliver the punchlines. When I ended, the hall erupted in loud applause.

The question and answer session began. Thankfully, Velu didn't ask a single question. The rest of the nine pitches went by like a blur. It was time for the bar to open and the fashion show to begin. I was talking to a few guys when Velu came in and warmly said hello to me. He asked if we could talk privately.

Velu began, 'Hey, you did good today. Well done.'

'Thanks, Velu. This event is very important for our success in Sri Lanka and getting the next round of funding and customers,' I said.

'Yeah, all the best, man.' He sipped his beer and then took a visible deep breath and said, 'Hey, I hope you will not remember the past and move on.'

I was relieved. 'Yes, don't worry about that. It's all water under the bridge.'

'That's great. See you then.' We shook hands and Velu left. The chilled beer suddenly started to taste better!

The fashion show ended, and the host came on stage to announce the winners. ThreadSol was adjudged the best start-up of the evening! I collected the large trophy and posed for all the whirring cameras. The day ended with 50+ business cards from investors from around a dozen countries and almost 50+ cards from the owners of various apparel manufacturing companies all around Sri Lanka. I shook hands with so many people that my hands were chaffed, and I received so many pats that I had a sore back.

In the end, I went back to the windowless Green Palace Inn where a loud wedding party was going on. The red-and-blue two-foot-tall trophy added another colour palette to Green Palace Inn's already colour-loaded room.

The next morning, when I was getting my sheets washed in the laundry next door, the owner of the laundry showed me my photo in the newspaper and asked for a selfie with me. I was a star! ThreadSol was a star!

By the latter half of 2014, we were getting a steady flow of wins in Sri Lanka and I spent three weeks a month in Colombo. That was when I said goodbye to the multi-coloured Green Palace Inn and rented a lovely 1,500 square foot fully furnished apartment, with wooden sloping roofs, in the heart of Colombo, Nugegoda, for $400 per month. Anas and Jaya would accompany me more often than not. Anas was learning the ropes of sales.

Jaya was a one-woman demolition squad. She spent 20 hours a day, seven days a week working. She would spend her days running trials in the Sri Lanka factories, travelling 4–5 hours a day, during which she would catch up on her sleep. At the Nugegoda flat, she spent her every waking hour either running the software and finding bugs and issues or working with her team in India to train them on the software and the trials and implementation nuances.

She was also taking care of the customers in Sri Lanka who were running our software, assisting them with queries and sorting out their concerns. She remained the nucleus of the project implementation and customer success team for the next five years until we sold the business. She helped set the processes and delivered some of the most critical projects for ThreadSol all around the globe.

The festival of lights, Diwali, was approaching. Everyone had gone back to Bangalore from Colombo and I had stayed back to complete one last deal. We were dealing with the Hirdaramanis. They owned a 20-factory consortium, headquartered in Colombo, and I had met them at the Sri Lanka Venture Engine start-up show. We implemented our software in their pilot factory. Jaya and Rohit did the implementation and it was a super success. They wanted to meet me to discuss a group-wide rollout and the meeting date was on Diwali.

The Hirdaramanis had come from India over 100 years back and set up businesses all around Sri Lanka. They owned 20 garment factories in Sri Lanka, Bangladesh and Vietnam. I went to their boardroom on the 33rd floor of the iconic World Trade Centre building in Colombo. In 40 minutes, we had signed a group deal of $500,000! I could not believe the number I was signing against – half a million dollars – wow! It was one of the biggest deals that ThreadSol would sign, and it came within one year of the first customer cheque of $15,000. This was a huge leap for all of us. When I sent the news on the ThreadSol WhatsApp group, the real Diwali fireworks took place there.

The meeting got over at 5.30 pm and I rushed to the airport to catch the 10 p.m. flight to Bangalore. I reached home at around 1 a.m. As I got to my apartment, I heard the sound of people talking loudly. This was strange. I was expecting to arrive to a quiet home – it was very late. When I entered, I saw 10 people sitting with their laptops on mattresses and the whiteboard, scrawled with numbers. The guys were discussing a technical problem and trying to come up with a solution at 1 a.m. on Diwali night!

As the night progressed, we all dived into the problem. Finally, by 3 a.m., we had a solution on the board that, to everyone's immense relief, Mausmi approved. Now, all we needed to do was to document this and send it to Abhishek and Bratish's team to build. The task of writing the algorithms and mathematics for the problem came on my plate. What a fun Diwali night!

After the team had left, Jaya wanted to speak to Mausmi and me. We sat down with a cup of tea on the balcony under a clear night sky.

'We have a problem,' Jaya started. 'It's about the new guy, Ajay. He is openly misogynistic. He has been misbehaving with Nikita, Silky and me. He has issues learning from female colleagues and is non-cooperative with women.'

Apparently, Ajay was raised in a household with seven sisters where he was pampered like a king. This was not unusual in Indian families and it had its unfortunate side effect of turning some of the young men in India into obnoxious sexists and misogynistic losers. They learnt and believed that women were inferior to men and it was manly to misbehave with them.

We all knew that India, as a society, had not done enough to protect its women to make them feel empowered to pursue economic freedom with dignity. But would ThreadSol do the same?

Mausmi and I were aghast to know the treatment Ajay was dishing out to our lovely ladies. We decided to dig deep into this. The next day, Mausmi spoke to all the women individually. They unanimously confirmed Jaya's story.

So, the day after Diwali, I bared my fangs. I fired Ajay, making it a public spectacle. I told him publicly that there was no way sexism and misogyny would be tolerated in ThreadSol. I told him that he was fired with immediate effect, that he would get one month's severance pay and that he had to leave right away. It was a publicly administered dishonourable discharge from duty – just like in the armed services.

After Ajay's departure, we four founders got into a huddle. We had to find a way to stop this from happening again. We looked into our experiences in past workplaces. Were they discrimination-free? No – they were not. Discriminations based on religion, race, gender, caste, colour, language, disability were rampant. They were accepted as the usual continuation of societal ills and never considered organizational problems. Yes, there were strong policies for anti-sexual harassment everywhere. However, discrimination in the form of daily, small-dosage-based retail harassments continued unabated in all organizations we had worked at.

We decided that we needed to make a stronger showing of our commitment. Thereafter, at every town hall, and to every new person who joined ThreadSol, I made it a point to say, 'If for any reason you cannot respect someone or cannot work with someone because you don't like their religion, caste, language, gender, race, sexual preference, food preferences, etc. please know I will be your worst nightmare and you will get a public dishonourable discharge.' I would then tell the Ajay story to them.

The incessant repetition did its trick and ThreadSol turned into a liberal and secular social order. Did we create shareholder value? Did our business succeed? Did we make enough money and have enough success? These were important considerations for the business. But, many of these things are never in the hands of the entrepreneurs. Setting up organizational culture and values, on the other hand, firmly lies with the founders. I am glad that we did very well in this department. No one in ThreadSol was ever a recipient of identity- and gender-based discrimination. I would count that as one of our biggest achievements.

Soon after that incident, Nikita had a new job on her desk. She wanted to find a tagline for ThreadSol that defined the company and represented what it stood for.

Jaya, Anas, Mausmi, Nikita, Kundan, Silky and I were discussing this, sitting in our Bangalore flat, when suddenly Rohit came in. He didn't care about the tagline discussion. He wanted to have golgappa and pushed us out of the flat to eat it.

A spectacular impromptu golgappa-eating competition ensued. Rohit, Anas and Kundan fought a three-way battle as Silky, Mausmi, Jaya, Nikita and I bowed out. The golgappas were vanishing thick and fast. At the 60-golgappa mark, Kundan bowed out. It was Anas vs Rohit. After 45 minutes of mayhem, Rohit emerged victorious with 72 golgappas!

The guy running the counter was so wiped out he went and sat on the street pavement, looking as if he was about to pass out. He had lost count!

Anas didn't take Rohit's victory too kindly.

'I will challenge you again. You may be the winner now, but you won't remain there for long,' he told Rohit.

Nikita jumped right in the middle of Anas' rant.

'Oooooh I know what our tagline should be, I know . . . I know . . . I know . . . Ooooh I know . . .'

We all looked at her and wondered what had gotten into her all of a sudden. Her five-foot frame shook in excitement.

'It should be "ThreadSol – Challenge the Present",' Nikita declared.

Nikita had nailed it!

'Challenge the Present' enshrined everything we were doing and aspired to do. Innovation is a challenge to the present status quo. It stuck and remained the tagline for the business. We loved it.

2014 drew to a close.

It was an awesome year. We had clocked $350,000 revenue with 30 per cent profits in 2014. Our team size was now 25; 15 had joined us that year. We had our foot firmly set in Sri Lanka. Bangladesh promised a lot. We also had ambitions for Vietnam, China and Turkey. We had two products now – IntelloCut and IntelloBuy – a true testament to the innovative spirit we wanted to inculcate in the organization.

To celebrate the perfect year, we all gathered in our Bangalore office. We had decided to leave Bangalore and move to Delhi again as most of our work was getting international and Delhi offered easier access to embassies for getting business visas.

We hired a bus and headed to the lovely hillside coffee plantation town of Coorg for a two-day off-site and camping. It was a terrific experience, and the highlight was a soul-bearing conversation that lasted nine long hours around a roaring bonfire. We looked like an ancient tribe that sat around a fire and told stories and invented their own rituals and painted their own mythical figures in the distant stars. A bonfire brings out the old caveman in all of us, and that night, the romance of the fire and the silent winter night created something magical.

The conversation was intense, with each person talking about how they saw ThreadSol and their colleagues and what they wanted from this journey. On that dark moonless night, in the faint flickering glow of the fire, you could see the burning ambitions in the eyes of a bunch of young 20-somethings – dreaming, aspiring and resolving to become a rock-solid group of people who were not afraid of the odds. They believed. And their collective belief gave four of us the biggest weapon of all – belief.

And with that, we welcomed 2015 – a year that would be one of the most important years of our journey, a year that would transform our humdrum hunter-gatherer ragtag band into a solid process and discipline-driven professional army; a year that would finally get us the love from the VC industry; a year that would take us into many new countries; a year in which we would use the newly garnered belief to expand our business to as many countries we could.

Let's go places . . .

14

Let's Go Places . . .

It was January 2015. The mood in the video call was grim.

Bratish's round face looked narrowed and pinched as he read out the news flash. Abhishek's forehead was furrowed with lines. Mausmi had gone ballistic with her blinking – a sign that she was agitated and nervous. And I had gone quiet.

'See Indian forces have claimed that the Pakistanis violated the Line of Control and fired at them, and in retaliation, Indian troupes fired back. The Pakistani forces are saying that the Indians were the aggressors. Both armies are claiming conflicting stories and a conflicting number of causalities. There is a lot of tension.'

'What are we going to do?' I asked.

'We should call the Ministry of External Affairs.' Abhishek said.

We all fell silent.

'Maybe, we should wait for another hour. Maybe there is some problem at the border, you never know . . .' Mausmi said.

The meeting ended on a sombre note with a decision to evaluate the situation in another hour.

Tensions with Pakistan on the border was not a new thing. But today, we had an issue. Our guy was crossing over to Pakistan and to make the matters worse, our guy had been untraceable for the last three hours. Our Pakistani business contacts facilitating his travel were unable to contact him too. We were all on edge. Did the Pakistanis take him for questioning? Was he imprisoned? Was he in trouble? What would we do? How long should we wait?

Saurav had joined ThreadSol a few months back. He was young, in his late twenties. He liked running, weight lifting and experimenting with diets to keep fit. He had worked in a few apparel businesses in the past. He needed the rigour of logic to believe anything and was not afraid to speak his mind. I liked his style of skepticism and his attention to detail.

I also admired his direct and no-nonsense attitude. We had to work hard to show him the logic and peel open all the layers of our innovation before he agreed with our philosophy. But once he was a convert, he was more than happy to become a missionary, spreading the light in the darkest regions of the world.

And what better place than Pakistan to ease him into this, huh? We had gotten in touch with a lovely Pakistani apparel software selling agency in Frankfurt. Kundan and Mausmi had connected with them at an international trade show there. The Pakistani agency invited us, and Saurav was our chosen evangelist. Being harder than a coffin nail, Saurav agreed.

He went through the harrowing visa process at the Pakistani Embassy. It is unbelievably complicated. You have to submit all your documents from school level until the date of application, all your income information, all your employers' information to date with reference, your current organization's complete details, the inviting organization in Pakistan and their complete details, the complete itinerary in Pakistan with a list of all cities that you have planned to go with the reason for the visit and the people you would meet.

Then the Pakistani Embassy will rigorously vet the person for one month. Finally, you get a Pakistani visa that will be valid for limited days and your visa will have names of the cities you are permitted to visit. Your visa will have pre-ordained details of the port of entry and exit. It is a very tight affair. It is almost impossible to go to our neighbouring country.

Saurav was crossing over to Pakistan for his 48-hour visit to Lahore at the Wagah border, 40 kilometres from Amritsar in India and 30 kilometres from Lahore in Pakistan. This was the border drawn by Sir Cyril Radcliff, who over the five weeks of work in July–August 1947, decided the boundary of India and Pakistan (and also East Pakistan, which later became Bangladesh in 1971).

The partition of India was one of the bloodiest exodus events in the world, where over 20 million people fled from one side to another, and almost two million died in the frenzied sectarian killings in just a few weeks. To put it in perspective, the US lost nearly 0.5 million civilians and soldiers in World War II. India and Pakistan were born out of this bloody strife, and the wound continues to fester over the dispute over the Indian territory of Kashmir. Enmity is the umbilical cord that conjoined the two nuclear powers that share the same language, music, arts, cuisine, cricket and political corruption for seven decades.

Just like India, Pakistan also has a thriving apparel industry and Saurav was on a two-day trip to convert a couple of accounts for ThreadSol.

Let's switch to Saurav's version for a better experience in understanding his story.

There were five–six people with me, crossing from India to Pakistan – all visiting relatives. The Indian side formalities were over very soon. We were escorted by the black Pathan suit-clad Pakistan Rangers to the Pakistani side's office building. I was singled out for special questioning as I was going for business purposes. Twenty minutes later, I was dropped at a no man's land by a battery-

powered rickshaw. This was the pick-up point where the hosts were supposed to collect the guests. My cell had stopped working and I had no network coverage. I spent almost two hours there, unable to inform my hosts to come and pick me up. Somehow, a Pakistani Ranger helped, and my hosts finally arrived.

The bustling metropolis of Lahore looked every bit like India except for the Urdu lettering in the shops and billboards. Our first stop was a mobile phone shop, where I got my local SIM card. As I was getting out of the shop, a black car pulled up and three men got out and walked towards me. A round of aggressive questioning ensued about why I was in Lahore. This was my first brush with the ISI. For the next 48 hours, they would never let me out of sight.

It was almost evening when I checked into my hotel. My hosts told me not to venture out alone at all. I had no plans of being so adventurous. Once I got into my room, I contacted my family and folks in India via WhatsApp. Everyone was tense as I had been off the grid for four hours. I laid their concerns to rest but didn't tell them about ISI. If I peeked from the heavy curtains of my window, I could see the black car standing in the hotel parking.

The next day, my hosts were at the porch and we drove straight to the meetings in the factories. The last meeting of the day turned out to be the most interesting one. The factory manager was an Indian hater. He agreed to everything I said and was nodding profusely to my pitch until someone told him that I had come from India. His volte-face was comical. He started disagreeing with everything from that moment onwards and told me that our software could never deliver savings in his factory as his processes were far better than the Indian factory processes.

I challenged him to a duel. His people could take half an order and execute it, and I would do the same with the other half using my software. The guy took the bait. It was 5 p.m. My hosts were worried. They wanted me to return to the hotel before nightfall, but I brushed them aside.

At 9 p.m., the factory manager had nowhere to hide. His jaw was on the floor.

IntelloCut had saved 2.7 per cent fabric. The two halves of the order were run side by side on two tables and the difference in the final results was unmistakable. On the table operated by their folks laid a big pile of wasted fabric – and on my side of the table was a full saved-fabric roll! I stood there quietly. I didn't have to utter a word to prove I had won – the technology and the innovation I was representing had won.

Everyone was impressed. The factory people were impressed. My hosts were impressed. Even the India-hating general manager was impressed. I was sure the ISI agents camping outside the factory and probably using their spy-grade parabolic mics to eavesdrop were also impressed.

The next day, I closed the deal. I guess profits trump nationalism!

As I was slated to return to India the next morning, my hosts took me out to the city for a night of fun and festivity. At night, you could mistake Lahore markets for Sarojini Nagar or Khan market. There was really no difference. People also looked the same – the old city could easily pass off as Chandni Chowk in Delhi or the Charminar area in Hyderabad. I had some exquisite Mughlai food. It was so good that I was blown away.

I was in a great mood. I had closed a deal of $60,000 on my first trip. When I was getting into the hotel through the heavy revolving door, I turned around and waved my ISI friends goodbye.

To date, Saurav downplays his first trip to Lahore in 2015. But I know he navigated a lot of landmines. I was convinced that he needed a bigger turf to play. And unsurprisingly, he made a bid for the same. He wanted to run Southeast Asia. And I gave him that. A superstar deserves a bigger banner movie.

In early February 2015, Saurav landed in Ho Chi Minh City,

Vietnam, for a two-week exploratory trip and began his work of spreading ThreadSol in Vietnam, Cambodia, Thailand, Laos, Philippines – just like the Christian missionaries had done in the early nineteenth century in Africa. His two-week exploratory trip extended to an unbelievable four years! The chap never came back except for the annual gatherings and occasional meetings. His stories from Southeast Asia are worthy of a book and I hope he will write them up someday. In the years he stayed in Vietnam, he did a bare-knuckle slog and delivered a million-dollar-plus revenue stream. In fact, Southeast Asia would deliver close to $3 million for us in the next four years! Saurav made his own team with local folks, prevailed over the complexities of language barriers and cultural biases and became one of the true superstars of ThreadSol.

Every time anyone asked him when he wants to come back to India, he would give a curt reply – 'I am going places.'

I still remember meeting Anas for the first time in 2012. At first glance, he came off as a typical arrogant brat from Delhi. He showed up in the interview with an unbuttoned shirt over a tee and torn denim with flip flops. He sat with an air of superiority and spoke to me as if he was doing me a favour by appearing for the interview.

It was the fall of 2012 and we had just gotten the confirmation of the seed investment intent from Blume. Mausmi and I had come to NIFT New Delhi to hire a few folks. This is where we met Anas for the first time.

'Let me make it abundantly clear to you that I will not work in manufacturing.' He told me.

I looked at this 22-year-old kid and wondered where he got

such guts from. Was this arrogance or was this brilliance wrapped in cockiness?

So, I gave him some seriously difficult problems to solve – let's see if you are a real deal or just a windbag.

'If you solve this, come back or don't bother.' I told him with a dismissive air. I was sure if he was the real deal, my disdainful treatment would push him to prove his worth.

Anas wrestled, struggled, huffed and puffed for half an hour or so and then came back again to see me. He had solved quite a few correctly and had made admirable progress in the rest.

We got three guys from NIFT New Delhi that day. Anas was on the list and I picked him for sales. He would go on to tour Sri Lanka with me. In the very first meeting, while I was setting up my laptop, I saw Anas duck under the table to connect the laptop charge cable to a power outlet.

'Never ever do this again.' I told him after the meeting.

'You are not my secretary. I want the customer to take you seriously. If you do menial jobs, how do you expect them to respect you?' Needless to say, Anas never did it again.

In my next meeting, I gave him the chance to lead the sales presentation. He bombed it and I took over. He had to sit and endure my presentation while he agonized. Anas was so pissed with himself that he remained silent like a grave for the entire two–hour car ride after the meeting. But he quickly bounced back and did a reasonable job in the next meeting as the presenter.

Soon he was running around in India trying to close sales. And India was treating him real bad. His ego was being punctured in every customer interaction. But he kept trying despite remaining winless. When I would return to Bangalore from Sri Lanka, with wins under my belt, I would see his face consumed in dark shadows. Indian customers grind you into pulp. I liked his pain. If you are hurting, then you want the wins that much more.

He put in herculean efforts into learning the software and spent hours and hours playing with it. He re-did the sales deck and practised it hard. Yet, he had nothing to show for his efforts. His counterparts like Kundan had closed deals in India, starting after him. That must have bruised his self-esteem a bit. Kundan went to Turkey to try and develop the business there. Anas was still running around in Delhi and Bangalore.

In the dying days of 2014, Anas came to me and opened up. 'Manasij, I don't want to do India. I am wasting my talents here.' He was direct and terse. 'Okay, why don't you take over Sri Lanka from me?' I said. 'You do Sri Lanka and I will move to Dhaka and open up the Bangladesh market for us.'

'No. I don't want Sri Lanka. It is yours. I want to build my own empire.' That's the usual cockiness Anas displayed!

'I want something that I will build from scratch and I will own. Give me Bangladesh.'

I thought about this for a moment. This guy hasn't sold a penny's worth of software in India. He didn't want to take the laid-out turf in Sri Lanka. He wanted to take up Bangladesh, the second-largest apparel manufacturing geography on the planet. I was best placed to take up Bangladesh. I had sold almost half a million dollars of software and I spoke fluent Bengali. And this guy wants to take on Bangladesh? Should I ask him to prove himself first in India and Sri Lanka? What should I do? Believe in him?

'Okay, Anas. Bangladesh is yours,' I said.

'Thanks. You will not regret this.'

When I communicated the decision to my co-founders, they were shocked. How could I give Bangladesh to Anas? Wasn't that supposed to be my cup of tea? But, just like I believed Anas, my folks believed me. We all knew Bangladesh would be tough. It was a difficult place. It was hard to live and work there. There was a lot of corruption and malpractice. Was Anas tough enough to stay in the hellhole and deliver? Would his natural flair and cockiness come in the way? Would he be able to build a team? There were too many unknowns. But we believed that Anas could do this.

In December 2014, Anas made his first trip to Bangladesh. We all waited with bated breath. Bangladesh was critical for our success. The moment of truth was upon us.

Within a month of him landing there, Anas closed his first deal. From 2015 to 2018, in four years, Anas and his sales team, which he created from scratch, would rake in close to $3 million in sales from the country.

In *John Wright's Indian Summers*, a fantastic memoir of his India cricket team coaching days, Wright remarks that, in his mind, Virender Sehwag was never out of form. He was always at his best. He always believed that he could dominate any bowler – that he could hit him out of the park any time. He believed in that with his heart and soul.

Sehwag may have had the fire but in the end, it was John Wright's and Saurav Ganguly's belief in him that made Viru the destructive force he was. Our belief in our team and our colleagues can transform them. Anas wanted to really, really win and our belief in him gave him the wind beneath his wings.

Dhaka, February 2015

Anas was sitting with an evil smile on his face.

'You will not last 10 minutes in a sales pitch, Manasij.' His voice was full of amusement.

'Really?' I was not impressed. 'Try me.'

'Okay, let's say you go to a sales meeting and the owner of the garment manufacturing firm asks you "Hey Manasij, you know Bangladesh is awarding the death sentence to the war criminals of the 1971 independence movement. What is your opinion?" What would you say?'

I was puzzled. 'Why would someone bring this up?'

'They can, right?' Anas was insistent.

'Yes, I suppose.' I had to concede. 'I will say it is a good thing . . . I guess?'

'Aaannnhhh . . .' Anas made the wrong answer buzzer sound and burst out laughing.

'See this guy was a sympathizer to the folks being hanged. So, you got burned. You just lost the deal dude.'

'Play again?' he asked.

'Yes.' I said.

'Okay, now let's say you go to meet another owner. You have shown them savings. They are happy. You feel you are doing good. So, you mention the name of this large denim unit who are using IntelloCut and getting great results. And then the meeting goes south. You end up with no deal. What just happened?'

I was perplexed. 'Did I offend him somehow?' I guessed.

'Duh . . . Obviously, you did.' He hit his forehead with his palm. 'The question is what was your mistake?'

'I don't know. What did I do?'

'Oh nothing, the other factory you mentioned, they patronize the opposition party and this guy patronizes the ruling one.' Anas was laughing.

I was speechless.

'Okay, okay. Here is another one. Suppose the same thing happens again, except the factory name you mentioned patronizes the same party that this guy patronizes. Yet, you lose the deal. Why?' He asked.

I was getting irritated. 'I don't know, dude. Maybe he doesn't believe in evolution and I do?'

'Well, this guy was defeated by the owner of the other factory you just mentioned in the last election for the secretary's post of their garment association. Wanna play more?'

'No, I want another coffee.'

I went to the café counter and ordered another mocha. This was my second trip to Bangladesh. Clearly, I had a lot of catching up to do.

The period of 2014–2015 was marked by terrible political turmoil. The two main political parties in Bangladesh, the Awami League (AL) led by Prime Minister Sheikh Hasina and the Bangladesh Nationalist Party (BNP) in opposition, led by three-time former prime minister Begum Khalida Zia, waged a fiery political battle. As I have described earlier, the streets were on fire. The country was being torn apart by the bitter rivalry between the two parties.

The apparel industry was severely impacted. This was Bangladesh's most important industry. Almost 80 per cent of the country's exports came from this sector and it had leapfrogged to become the second-biggest apparel manufacturing destination in the world after China.

The media was owned by the apparel industry moguls, who also controlled banks and real estate and, in some cases, arms exports and the drug industry too.

Apparel was the biggest buck of Bangladesh and its associations ran a parallel government that had all the powers and political connections. With money came the power to back political parties; therefore, when the battle lines were drawn, it opened deep fissures in the industry as well.

Since their factories were run in a feudal manner and the owners ruled as dictators (corporate structure was rare here), we had to deal with their likes and dislikes, their idiosyncrasies. Without any on-ground intel on their political affiliations and their background, we couldn't hope to make progress. No amount of sales training would work without on-ground intel. When it came to Bangladesh, it was truly the Wild Wild East!

Let me give you Anas' viewpoint in his voice:

I had come to Bangladesh after my sales learnings in Sri Lanka and partly India. Here, they meant nothing. My first meeting was over in 15 minutes as I made an error in taking a political side. In another meeting, the owner kept talking about the increasing gas prices, asking if I could do anything with my software to solve his heavy gas bill.

On another occasion, the guy kept asking me how I felt as a Muslim in India. One more meeting turned out to be a washout when the owner told me to sell the software for $15,000 and he threatened that if I didn't do so, he could ensure I would never get out of Bangladesh. It shook me a bit, but I moved on. One owner kept talking about food and asked me if I had tasted the delicious Bengali sweets. When I told him I had not, he arranged for five kilograms of sweets to be sent to my hotel! After the first three months, all I had was abrupt endings to promising meetings and a box of sweets weighing five kilograms!

On top of all this, the logistics were extremely cumbersome. There was no Uber or other app taxis. The radio taxis had a wait time of over one hour. The autorickshaws were the most abundant, but they were claustrophobic tin cans and, in the heat and humidity of Dhaka, a real hazard. Traffic in the city was terrible. It took one hour to travel five kilometres. In a day, I was spending six–seven hours on the road to do two meetings. There was terrible unprofessionalism all around. Meeting times were so fluid that one could never do more than one meeting before lunch and another after. I was unable to close deals.

And the lawlessness around me was terrifying. I could see open buying and selling of petrol bombs, and once, I took photos of these and posted them in the ThreadSol WhatsApp group. I got so many calls of concern from my buddies that I never posted another security hazard report anywhere. Sometimes at night, I could see flames in distant buildings and wondered if, one day, my hotel could be attacked.

Amid all of these, I had a meeting with the owner of a manufacturing group. The owner was a man in his mid-forties, educated in the US and had inherited the family business. He met me with his coterie in his resplendent top-floor office, with a helipad on the roof. He looked like a classic Bond villain. He sat in a huge office and had a giant 80 inches' LCD monitor in front of him where he could see hundreds of small rectangles playing live video feed from all over his factory.

He had a gargantuan crystal globe and he liked spinning it while talking to the people. Everything was covered in white leather with red, exposed stitching. He smoked incessantly and spoke to everyone in a demeaning manner. The only thing missing was a vixen by his side. He had his middle-aged big-bearded COO instead.

I don't know why, but I began with, 'Let me tell you, your fabric planning is pathetic.'

The guy sat up on his chair. I copied his style and spoke with a heady mix of my value-driven sales pitch and a condescending tone. He was impressed. Sensing an upper hand, I decided to go for broke and asked for a cigarette from him. So, here I was, in the brute's office, smoking with him while he barked orders to implement our software and get the CFO to sign the deal! I had my first deal in Bangladesh and learnt a valuable lesson – only the tough vegetation survives in these predatory soils.

When Manasij came in February 2015, I had a couple of deals lined up. I had also signed a reseller for our software. I was sure that Bangladesh, despite its oddities, could deliver big. I needed a bigger team and a permanent outpost here. But before I asked for these, I had to give Manasij a taste of the local cuisine. So, I took him to this popular Nordic Bakery in the Gulshan area and gave him a Bangladesh sale 101. It worked. He realized this place was different and needed a different touch.

I stirred my mocha and reflected on the conversation I had just had with Anas. What I knew from my experiences was not applicable here. So I gave Anas what he wanted. He could find a place in the Gulshan area of Dhaka to live and build his team here. He had shown enough resolve to deserve this. We celebrated our decision with some lovely Irish Cream. I had no idea the same bakery would be the theatre of a bloody hostage crisis and a massacre 18 months later where two dozen people would lose their lives.

But Bangladesh was always different. I remember in 2015 end, I was visiting Bangladesh for a few days for a marketing event. By then, Anas and his team had worked hard to warm up a large denim manufacturer to sign a $100,000 deal with us. The managing director (MD) was primed to sign the deal. However, one of the factory general managers was baulking and was employing a painful blocking tactic.

He claimed that his factory personnel were unable to understand the product demo because of the language barrier. He wanted the product demo in Bangla to convince the guys. The MD asked Anas to officiate a demo in Bangla. As Anas and his team didn't speak Bangla, the deal was getting delayed and risked cooling off. As any enterprise sales go, if a deal cools off, re-warming is a very tall order.

When I arrived in Dhaka, Anas raised the subject. 'Look Manasij, I want this freaking deal done.' He exhaled a huge cloud of smoke and flicked the ash of his lit cigarette on the ground.

'I need your help. And if you do exactly like I tell you, we will have this deal in our hands. What do you say?' He looked at me.

"Okay. What do I need to do dude?' I asked.

'We will go to the factory headquarters tomorrow. The MD and the factory general manager are going to be present with a few guys from their factory. These chaps speak Bengali. You will do the demo in Bengali for these guys.' He paused and added, 'Mind you, I will not introduce you as the CEO. I won't introduce you at all. You cannot give them your name or your card. You will do the demo and answer their questions in Bengali and that's where your role ends. I will close the deal. In case they ask for your name, just say you are Manasij – that's all. Good enough?' He asked.

'Sure, let's do this. I am in,' I said.

I was amused. This looked like fun.

The next morning, we dressed up. Anas looked chic in his jacket and tie. I was asked to wear only a shirt and tie and no jacket to underscore Anas' seniority. We hired a pedal-powered rickshaw. If the meetings were close by, it made sense to take the rickshaw than a car. The traffic in Dhaka was probably the world's worst. The rickshaw guys knew many narrow lanes and they could zoom from one part to another in the shortest possible time.

And they were cheap too. However, we had to alight from the rickshaw a full block away from the factory's headquarters. It would have looked bad for our image to arrive at a meeting in a rickshaw. Dhaka is a very class-conscious society and we had no intention of looking like a company with limited means, especially when we were about to do a $100,000 deal with these guys.

The meeting started one hour late – it was not unusual in Dhaka to have such delays. Anas led the sales conversation. He sat at the round table with the MD and general manager. I sat in a cluster of chairs with half a dozen Bengali workers, away from the bosses and waiting for the appropriate juncture. My moment came some 30 minutes into the meeting. Anas didn't bother to introduce me. The half a dozen workers were also left unintroduced. The workers didn't protest – that's how hierarchal a society it was.

I put my head down and did a one-hour demo plus a question and answer session in Bengali with the workers. I stopped when Anas wanted me to stop, for him to emphasize a point or two with the bosses and I resumed when I was commanded. It was all good. They were happy. The MD and the manager were happy. I was happy. We were shown the door and I waited at the reception. Anas stayed behind, seated at the round table with the bosses, to close the deal.

He emerged with the bosses in another 30 minutes. I didn't want to ask about the outcome of the meeting, so we walked out of the building silently. We turned the corner so that we could no longer be seen by anyone from the office building. Then we both burst into a fit of laughter, high-fiving each other in the middle of the busy Dhaka street. The deal was ours. Anas had closed it. I had played the part of an unnamed, insignificant Bengali-speaking product-demonstration guy and Anas, the 23-year-old, played my boss and got us the $100,000 deal!

Before I left Dhaka, something funny happened. Anas had signed a reseller for us in Bangladesh and the reseller invited us to the biggest apparel trade show in Dhaka to participate with them. The same reseller represented some other bigger respected names in the apparel machinery and software space. They had made high-quality arrangements for the 'principals' – the companies he represented. The senior representatives of all the principals were to sit on a comfy chair near the pizza oven that the reseller had erected in the trade show stall!

I was the CEO of ThreadSol; therefore, I had a place in the high chair. As I was ushered to my seat, I saw a familiar face. The familiar face also saw me and the light from his face just vanished. I extended my palm and shook his limp hand warmly.

'Hey Bill, this is Manasij again. Hope you recognize me?'

He nodded wryly. He was looking grim.

Two years ago, in Shanghai, during the CISMA show in 2013, it was Bill who had kicked me out of the Gerber stall. The same guy who had publicly humiliated me was now sharing the dais with me as equals in Dhaka!

If a different time and a different place make so much of a difference, then heck – let's go places . . .

Istanbul, Bangkok, Jakarta, Manila, Hanoi, Dhaka, Colombo . . .

The year 2015 saw ThreadSol make inroads in these places. We had the first deals coming from each of these cities. The stories were similar. Our evangelical emissaries had shown exemplary fortitude in carrying our innovation flag to multiple foreign shores.

By now, I was travelling like a madman. I would spend a week in Noida and then travel for weeks, going all over South Asia, Southeast Asia, the Middle East, Europe and sometimes the US. My passport pages were running out at a breakneck pace, and I was starting to feel familiar with some of these cities. In fact, you could say I ran ThreadSol on the road.

I learnt some tricks through the crazy travelling. For instance, I only always travelled with hand luggage. Every time you check in luggage, you add 30–40 minutes extra in the airport and I was taking 200 flights a year – that would work out to four days of waiting for luggage! I was surprised when in one of the inflight movies I watched *Up in the Air*, the character Ray Bingham, played by the dashing George Clooney made the exact point!

The only difference was his character always flew business class, whereas to save money, I was always in economy class. Barring a few lucky trips, I was never upgraded to business class. I had also optimized my wardrobe for speed and efficiency. I carried two pairs of denim, five black tees and one semi-formal jacket for all meetings. A pair of sneakers was good enough for all travel and meeting purposes. This was enough for me to power through a 10-day itinerary that would include three–four cities.

I had become addicted to the pacy life and the frequent hops into the aeroplanes and trips to the airports didn't bother me so much. My daily meals were always from McDonald's, Pizza Hut, Domino's, Burger King, etc. I had grown to tolerate the familiar food that was guaranteed to not make me get any bugs. Sometimes, after closing a big deal or after a hectic week, I would treat myself to some good food. Steaks, Korean barbecues, sushi and sashimi and Spanish tapas were my favourites.

My new travel habits pointed to a bigger business reality – it was clear that our innovation was a global play. It had to now expand and that needed capital for the expansions. It was quite evident to me that it was time to start looking for the next round of investments from VC firms again!

So, I dusted my cape, sharpened my sword and jumped on my noble stead's back to embark on the heroic quest for capital. The last six months of 2015 were spent all on the road, trying to raise funds for ThreadSol. It turned out to be as painful as trying to raise the first round of funding. Finally, the jinx was broken by one of India's biggest tech luminaries, the legendary founder and technocrat par excellence Narayana Murthy.

It once again underscored something critical about the Indian VC scene – the niche needs a visionary and no VC.

15

Niche Needs a Visionary and No VC

The fifth of July 1687 was a red-letter day in history. It was the day when the most influential scientific book of all time, *Philosophiæ Naturalis Principia Mathematica* by the legendary Sir Isaac Newton, was published. The book answered the age-old question of how the universe worked and mathematically explained the motions of the stars, planets, the Sun and the Earth. The book unleashed the dawn of modern sciences and Newton is forever immortalized as a person sitting under the proverbial apple tree, waiting for the apple to fall on his head!

However, the man who stood behind is less well known. Edmund Halley was a brilliant mind – an astute astronomer, a brilliant meteorologist – and a consummate mathematician. His work of charting the trade winds and monsoon was a landmark. The symbols and notations he used for the study of trade winds are still in use today. But his most significant contribution was identifying the genius of Newton.

He saw young Newton's work and believed in it so much that he gambled most of his wealth into getting Newton's book published. The book went on to become an international hit and catapulted Newton's standing to a megastar. But if it was not for Halley backing him, who knows if Newton would have gotten the same adulation. Alas, the world remembers Edmund Halley for the only thing he did not discover – Halley's Comet, which visits the Earth roughly every 76 years. Halley calculated the time it took for this comet to reappear and people remember him after this heavenly body.

Spotting talents and opportunities and backing them with wealth is not new. Roman impresarios used to roam countries in search of worthy gladiators and they would put an enormous amount of effort and money to find them. Merchants backed invaders with money so that if the invasion succeeded, they would be given favourable business rights. Empires have financed expeditions to the farthest corners of the world, in search of riches – be it silk, ivory, gold, silver, tea, slaves. Powerful Western nations have put money into banana republics to instil their puppet governments in the hope of controlling strategic mineral wealth.

The modern VC industry, however, is way more sophisticated than the examples given earlier but no less chaotic. The business model of a VC firm is quite simple. VCs bet on start-ups and take up equity stakes (part ownership of the company) in lieu of capital. They hope that the start-up they bet on will grow big and their equity will be valued manifolds. Typically, a VC firm is started by a small group of managing partners. These guys are connected to wealthy people from whom they raise money.

Let's say two colleagues who were once hotshot Wall Street bankers get together as managing partners, create a VC firm and raise $100 million from wealthy folks. Once someone invests money in a VC firm, they are called limited partners (LPs). The VC firm has to return a 'carry interest' of say 20 per cent to the LPs.

The fund horizon is typically six to eight years – so, in that timeframe, they need to return the LPs the money with the carry interest. Now, the VC firm needs to have an office and hire a few analysts from the top B-schools. They also hire some mid-level principals and some senior partners who are experienced in the VC game and can help in future fundraises and spot the winning start-ups. All of this costs money. So, the VC firm charges a small management fee (typically 2 per cent) of the total money raised to do the housekeeping. That way, the VC firm that has raised $100 million has $2 million to run and manage the business.

Typically, the analysts are the lowest-rung players in the VC firm. They are paid salaries and they do all the leg work of analysing and pondering over details pertaining to numbers, plans, data, etc. They advise the principals. The principals are the people who mostly interact with the new start-ups to spot opportunities and if they like something, they pass it to the analysts for a detailed review.

Once the review is positive, they kick the opportunity upstairs to the partners, and if the partners like the opportunity, this goes to the Investment Committee (IC). The IC is the final body that decides if the investment is a go-no-go. The IC generally has the managing partners, the senior partners and a few principals. If the IC likes the opportunity, it sends the start-up a term sheet. This is an investment-intent document. The start-up and the VC firm discuss this and strike a deal.

Let's say the VC firm likes a start-up. And they decide to invest $1 million into the start-up at a post-money valuation of $10 million. This means the VC firm owns 1/10 = 10 per cent of the start-up. Now, for simplicity's sake, let's assume the start-up does not raise any more money and runs a runaway successful business and five years later, is bought by Google at, say, $300 million valuation. Now, because the VC firm owned 10 per cent of the start-up, they make 10 per cent of the $300 million = $30 million! The VCs generally get paid first if any trade sales happen.

The payout structure in VC firms is also quite fascinating. The managing partners have a carry interest in almost all deals that the VC firm would strike. This means, out of the $30 million deal mentioned above, once the LPs are paid, the managing partners have the first claim in cashing their carry interest (typically 20–25 per cent) on the deal. Then the senior partner who carried the deal cashes in. Generally, the principals don't cash in at every deal level and they get yearly bonuses. The analysts mostly just lick their wounds.

The above case, where a $1 million initial investment returns $30 million, is considered a huge success, and wealthy LPs will notice that the VC firm is particularly good at spotting start-up opportunities, and they'll make a beeline to buy into the VC firms' funds. So, the VC firm will launch a second round of fundraising and raise say $500 million. And the cycle repeats.

However, such unbelievable successes are rare. Most start-ups end up in flames and the money invested into them sinks forever. That is why the VC business is risky. However, without VC money, start-ups can rarely grow and deliver big wins. Since the whole ballgame is so messy and mostly driven by the gut, it gives rise to cycles of violent boom and bust, euphoria and despair.

The industry shows classic signs of summit fever – i.e. a sudden urge to undertake an extremely challenging and potentially life-threatening endeavour without thinking it through, just because many are doing it, something the professional mountaineers know all too well and actively dissuade from.

In the VC world, it is called FOMO – Fear of Missing Out. If many VCs start investing in, say, dog-walking start-ups, the others get this bout of FOMO and they rush into investing in another dog-walking start-up (believe it or not, it is a real thing and VCs have invested in it). The VCs find it irresistible to sink their teeth into the juicy world of fads.

The Indian VC funding scene is a $8–$10 billion-a-year gig. And it is controlled by no more than 50 super-strong individuals who rule the largest war chests. You hear their bytes, read their tweets, see their interviews all the time. Unless you meet the right guys, there is no hope for your story to get wings. The VC firms are mini fiefdoms where the lowly functionaries have no real say in decision-making.

The year 2015 was a watershed period in VC funding in India. The bull run of the valuations for Ola, Zomato, Swiggy, Flipkart, Paytm, Snapdeal, Shopclues, etc. was in full swing. Money was being invested at a breakneck pace. There were a lot more start-ups in the market and the clamour for VC funding was rising to feverish pitches.

This was a great time to be a VC. There were too many great opportunities, and it was like shooting fish in a barrel. For the start-ups, it was hard going. There was a lot more competition and the VCs could afford to wait and watch and pick winners. For start-ups, time is an enemy. The more time passes, the harder it gets to scale without cash and that starts a negative reinforcement loop with the VCs until the start-up ends up being roadkill under the wheels of a well-funded competitor or an anonymous death with nothing left but ghost Twitter handles, ghost websites and the ghosted dreams of the founders.

~

The ThreadSol story was good. We had grown from $30,000 in revenues in 2013, to $350,000 in 2014, and in 2015, it looked like we would do $1.3 million. We had dizzying growth and we were net profitable – a near-impossible feat in the start-up world. We were in a territory with almost zero competitors and a large international market with two products that had demonstrable product-market-fit. All good.

However, I harboured the ambition of growing faster. Yes, we could have taken it slow and used the proceeds of the profits to grow the business. But that would be slow. And that would not curry favour with the investors on my board. The VCs need to see rapid growth and a rapid uptick in valuation to justify to their investors.

Once you take money from VCs, you are committed to playing this game – there is no turning back. We had reached the coveted million-dollar revenue mark in 18 months from the first customer cheque – that's blazingly fast. However, we needed to make the leap to the next marker of $5 million. We estimated a raise of $3 million would take us there. This will largely go into sales and marketing and a sizable portion into the technology side as well. So, I had to again get on the road to raise capital.

But we were in the apparel tech domain – a domain that did not exist and therefore had no VC attention whatsoever. It would be hard to get the VCs to look at us when they are driven by FOMO and fads and have favourite sectors for investment. We had to find a spark to get into the limelight. So, I played the card that had given us the results the last time around. I went back to the marketing team for help.

ThreadSol marketing was being run by Wilson Lobo – a six-foot, weighing about a 100 kilograms, solidly built, long-haired, tattooed dude, who had joined us recently. Wilson and Nikita were setting up the marketing processes fast and experimenting with many angles. So, when I realized that I need to look more attractive than just numbers on a spreadsheet, I went back to Wilson and Nikita for help.

In no time, they fashioned up an investor campaign and as a result, I had meetings on my calendar with Accel, Sequoia Capital, Nexus Venture Partners, Matrix Partners, SAIF Partners, Kalaari Capital and Lightspeed. Blume Ventures, our seed round investors, pitched in with more introductions and I had my calendar full. For a change, I was again flying domestic and having meetings in Mumbai and Bangalore and Delhi with the investors.

The investors liked our terrific growth and loved the fact that we also posted net profits. But, they were hesitant to bet on apparel tech. There were no success stories in the US and China in the area and that was somehow construed as clinching evidence of this being a sector that was 'not that hot'. Some of the investors came to see our product in action in the factories of Raymond suiting and Blackberry shirts and left impressed, but we were still far from anyone committing to invest in us.

'Yeah, we like you guys, but I think we would want to wait and watch a little longer.'

'We don't invest in this type of tech now. Keep up the growth and we might look at you in a few years.'

'Can you not sell your products in the US? That would have helped us validate you better.'

'Why has no one in China built something like this?'

'Is the apparel sector that big? Wow, we had no idea.'

'This is too much of a niche for us.'

'That's impressive growth. You also have profits. Wow! We like you, but . . .'

We were looked upon with intrigue, but with a view that this was a business that could not be VC-backed.

By the time September 2015 rolled in, over 50 VC funds had met with us and rejected our investment proposal. It started to look as if despite ticking all the boxes in growth, product-market fit, profits, etc. the maverick status of apparel tech was our Achilles heel. While it is possible to grow business by banking on the profits from it, the growth would surely be slower.

The constant rejections were taking a toll on all four of us founders. In the initial days, we would discuss the VC meetings with zeal, and then with time our enthusiasm waned and we started to realize that we might not be able to raise money after all. However, it never deflated us. As I was the person at the forefront of the fundraising, I bore the brunt of the rejections, and Abhishek, Bratish and Mausmi were always supportive. My colleagues were treating me great while the VCs were dishing out one negative after another.

On the other hand, some of our happy customers were asking us if they could invest in us. Hirdaramani group, who had done a $500,000 group deal with us last year, wanted to invest $300,000 if we could find a lead investor. The CEO of Li & Fung (a 40-billion-dollar apparel sourcing business based in Hong Kong) had suggested this too. Blume Ventures, our existing seed round investors were happy to join the fundraising too.

Building and growing a start-up depends on three important variables: one, the execution of the business by the founders; two, the hospitability of the market to sustain the growth; and three, the horsepower of the investors to make scaling the business smoother and faster. We had the first two firmly showing positive trends.

Clearly, we needed a visionary investor and someone who had serious guts to back us. Just like Newton needed Edmund Halley, we needed someone who understood steely business execution.

My first opportunity came in 2015 September when our marketing team's perseverance bore fruit and I was chosen as one of the top 50 coolest start-up CEOs in India at a glittering function in the Taj Hotel, Bangalore. Ex-Infosys chairman Mohandas Pai was giving away the awards. He had the reputation of being an indomitable, outspoken, gritty investor and I felt he could get behind our story. The problem was I had no way to reach Pai and the event was being attended by over 5,000 people and some 500 founders wanted to speak to him, just like I did.

As I wandered around the sprawling manicured lawn of the Taj, an interesting game plan crystallized in my head. What if I didn't reach out to Mohandas Pai, but got him to reach out to me? I went to the event organizers and asked them if they could change the one-minute introduction that our marketing team had sent to them.

Before every awardee was called upon the stage to receive the award and click the customary photo with Mohandas Pai, the organizers would read out the one-minute introduction. That was my opportunity to put my plan in motion. To my immense relief, the organizers agreed and I gave them a new introduction and went back to the hall.

The event began. There were customary speeches lauding the Indian start-up scene and then the award show began. I was restless. I had played a gambler's hand. Would that work?

'In the SaaS solution for the world of manufacturing category, we present Mr Manasij Ganguli of ThreadSol the coolest CEO award for scaling ThreadSol to a dizzying 400 per cent growth with 30 per cent net profit margin to seven countries in just 18 months.' The announcer read out my 10-second introduction as opposed to a long one-minute introduction and as the 35,000 watts of booming music took over, I walked slowly on stage to accept my award from Pai.

As we stood beside each other for the photo-op, he leaned over and whispered in my ear, 'What do you do?'

'Shall we discuss it at the dinner?' I replied.

'Yes, let's talk,' he said.

I climbed down from the dais with my award in my hand and with a bigger smile on my face.

ThreadSol was the only awardee where what the company did was not mentioned in the introduction – the short intro focused only on its fast growth. My aim had been to let the numbers intrigue the media and the VCs and not dilute the message with anything else. Thankfully, my gamble worked!

As soon as the award show was over, Mohandas Pai was swarmed by hundreds of eager founders and journalists as I waited patiently in the flanks but within his line of sight. After a few minutes, he gestured to me to come over. We escaped the crowds and sat down in the cordoned-off area for the VIPs and had a detailed chat and he gave me the contacts of his investment fund colleagues to contact. Before I left the venue, I had a meeting fixed with his VC fund managers! Things move quickly when you play smart and the top guy blesses you!

After dinner, I went to UB City where Karthik of Blume had invited me over for a coffee. Karthik was pleased to see us win the award and I told him about the evening's development. He immediately picked up his phone and connected me to Catamaran Ventures – the family money-driven VC fund headed by Infosys founder Narayana Murthy.

'See if you can convince the Infosys luminaries.' He laughed as I sipped my hot chocolate. I have always liked Karthik for his honesty and candour, and he and Blume are well known for being extremely founder-friendly and empathetic. This connection was going to become a pivotal point in our journey.

~

It was the day before Diwali in 2015. This was the third Diwali in ThreadSol's life. During 2013's Diwali, we had completed our first two deals giving us $29,000 in total and on the following year's Diwali, I had closed a group deal with the Hirdaramani Group for $500,000. This 2015 Diwali day was also proving to be crucial.

Mausmi and I were in the lovely leafy neighbourhood of J.P. Nagar in Bangalore where Infosys founder Narayana Murthy's family fund Catamaran Ventures had a beautiful office. Despite his multi-billionaire status, Narayana Murthy preferred being driven around in an eight-year-old Scorpio SUV and we could see it parked in the compound.

'Okay guys, your lives are about to change,' Rounak said in a serious tone.

'Yes, Narayana Murthy is a tough guy and he understands things very fast and if you guys fumble and stumble, it won't be good,' Abishek added.

Abishek managed the Catamaran Ventures and Rounak was the principal for our deal. We were supposed to meet Narayana Murthy for a final discussion on the investment offer from them. If he blessed us, we would get a term sheet and the $3 million investment would be ours to take.

We were in talks with Catamaran for over a month now and they had expressed a strong interest in investing with us. At the same time, the other VC fund that Mohandas Pai had connected us to was also interested. Both discussions were going in parallel. It is not unusual for an entrepreneur to have parallel funding discussions with the VCs and it helps to choose the most favourable deal on offer. We were in the final stages of both open discussions.

As we descended the winding staircases from the second floor to the ground floor, we were constantly being advised by the duo, Rounak and Abishek.

'Don't be tongue-tied in front of Narayana Murthy.'

'Don't talk a lot.'

'Be original and authentic.'

'Sound deep and thoughtful. NRM (that's what they call him) loves that.'

'Most entrepreneurs who meet NRM, tell us that the meeting changed their lives.'

Once we reached the ground floor, we made our way to the meeting room. I was looking at my phone as Kundan was texting me from China about the status of an important deal in Xingjian province. Big mistake.

Before I realized what had happened, I hit my forehead very hard on the ground and saw my flailing arms at my eye level. I had fallen straight through an open manhole and the only thing that saved me was my outstretched arms. Some workmen immediately pounced on me and pulled me out from the watery grave that lurked beneath. I had bruises all over my upper body and deep cuts on my left shin.

After receiving some first aid, I joked, 'Hey Rounak, you said entrepreneurs claim that meeting NRM changes their lives, I was about to lose mine.'

We got to the meeting. It was in a drawing room and Narayana Murthy was waiting for us, sitting in a comfortable chair. He stood up and greeted us, 'Hi, I am Narayana Murthy.'

I thought he looked shorter than what the photographs suggested. He also had worn his watch over his shirt. He had a piercing glance and spoke very slowly but clearly.

The meeting began on a super formal note where Abishek quickly introduced us. The Catamaran folks were a bit nervous in front of NRM and Rounak dropped his laptop while he started to explain what ThreadSol did and why they had chosen us to meet him to discuss the investment. Narayana Murthy stopped him and looked at Mausmi and said, 'Maybe you can explain your business to me?'

Mausmi explained what we did and then he nodded in appreciation and said, 'You know very few people know that the first software I ever developed was for a garment manufacturing company here in Bangalore.' And then he went about telling us of his experiences with the garment and apparel industry.

The tone of the meeting changed and Mausmi and I began an open and easy interaction with him. We even cracked a few jokes

– something we were asked to refrain from. It was clear he had deep insights into the businesses and was a very intelligent person.

An hour later, we came out of the meeting and as we jumped into our cab to get to the airport, Abishek gave us a thumbs up and said, 'We will let you know what's the internal decision.'

Mausmi and I reached Delhi airport way past midnight. We were tired after the whole day's running around in Bangalore and my lucky escape from a watery end. As I switched on my phone, I saw two emails. One was from Catamaran with the investment term sheet and the other was from the VC fund of Mohandas Pai – also with a term sheet of investment.

Wow . . . We had two VCs interested in investing $3 million into us. Back in 2015, a $3 million series A investment was considered pretty good. We were valued at $10 million by the investors, which is 10x of the revenue we were making – great from 2015 standards.

As the taxi zoomed past the near vacant Delhi streets, the night before Diwali fireworks added to the euphoria we were experiencing. All the hard work of all our people – all had finally paid off. It was 'Happy Diwali' for us three years running!

~

In the next two weeks, we had hectic meetings and negotiations with both the VCs to understand and negotiate terms. Karthik and Ashish from Blume created an unbelievable back-channel helping hand to keep all the parties happy. It was like keeping multiple pieces moving on an ever-changing chessboard.

'Play fair, Manasij. That's the first principle.' Karthik would tell me, in his usual baritone voice and earnest tone.

'But don't be shy to dig your heel in for getting a better deal. But you cannot be perceived as someone who is playing one player against another.'

And that was mighty tough. When you have more than one competing offer at hand, it is easy to go overboard in the euphoria and upset both parties to a point where they back out. I was playing that role. I would be lying if I said I did not enjoy it, but it was not something that would keep me kicked. In the end, we reached a point where both the VCs had given us 100 per cent identical offers. There was nothing to choose between them based on the term sheet! We had to choose one. But how? How do you choose when you have two exact same offers?

Luckily for us, Karthik and Ashish were visiting Noida at that time and they trekked up to ThreadSol's office and we caught up over some nice tea and snacks. The atmosphere was upbeat. It was one of those meetings that left a long impression on me and I recall almost the whole meeting in entirety.

'See guys, ultimately you got to understand that there are three pillars of success for any start-up. One is the entrepreneurial horsepower that the founders would bring in with their innovation, knowledge, erudition, instinct, execution, etc. Second is the market and every market has its own unique fingerprints of its level of acceptance for innovations, and that, in turn, dictates the speed limits of growth. And finally, third, the capital you are able to raise and from whom.'

Whenever Karthik would have a deep thoughtful speech to deliver, he would lean back in his chair, cross his legs and would look up at the ceiling. Ashish, on the other hand, would look you straight in the eyes and then articulate his views. We all respected their views a lot.

'See, the area in which you guys operate, apparel tech, is not a strong-laid technology vertical. So, it is, in a way, a category-creation activity. And category creation is hard, long and expensive. Therefore, you need to choose a VC that you feel more confident in helping you with a long-term patient viewpoint for creating a differentiated category.

You can look at many examples around us. Zomato was a category creator in India, and Sanjeev, the founder of Nakuri.com, backed Zomato for many rounds of funding. Mostly, he himself invested before anyone else could come into the fundraises. Similarly, RailYatri, a start-up that caters to the commerce around train travel, was continuously funded by Nandan Nilekani. And see where these two companies have reached.' And then Karthik delivered the line that stays with me till today. 'Niche needs a visionary and no VC.'

And we made our choice. We decided that we would ride on the visionary capabilities of Narayana Murthy to build ThreadSol. By November 2015, when we touched a $1 million sales figure for the financial year, we signed the definitive investment agreement with Catamaran Ventures. Hirdaramani, one of our customers, joined in and so did the CEO of Li & Fung Logistics, and Blume played their pro-rata part.

There were two small hurdles before the money came in. One, we had to relocate our business HQ to Singapore as almost 99 per cent of our revenue was international and we would have a much better stab at building an international business from Singapore and two, there would be a very quick round of due diligence (DD) that E&Y (one of the four largest consulting and auditing firms of the world) would do on ThreadSol to make sure everything was in order. This was expected to take four weeks. Rounak from Catamaran became our point man.

Life was good. We were about to get $3 million (almost ₹20 crore) in investment to grow our business. We would be headquartered at Singapore. We would be able to grow faster. Everything looked like it was starting to fall into place.

We expected the money to hit our bank in four weeks by the close of December, as promised by E&Y and Catamaran. So, off we went to Goa to celebrate the end of a fantastic year for ThreadSol.

The evening before we went to Goa, we kept an all-you-can-drink-bar sponsored by Abhishek. It was a wild evening of fun and drunken laughter and dancing. The next morning, 50 of us boarded a flight to Goa all wearing the same ThreadSol hoodie. Every hoodie had the person's name and a hashtag that defined them. The hashtags were chosen through popular voting among many crowd-sourced options.

My hashtag was #SmartCEO – an ode to the Smart CEO award that I had gotten. Abhishek got #KootDenge (will thrash you) – a term he often used when someone in the development team made a boo-boo in the code. Bratish got #IHave32Points – to commemorate the spirit of diligence he had shown for every meeting. Mausmi got #WonderWoman – probably because she knew everything about every division of the business and was the chief troubleshooter.

Some interesting ones read #BestStories for Rohit – for his penchant for starting stories really well and never delivering a climax or a punch line. #HighLife for Kundan for his penchant for spending carelessly. #FeatureNotBug for Kamal, the tech guy who would get into the hairs of the testing team by telling them that the bugs they logged were actually a feature of the product. This would become an annual ritual for us to go to a two–three-day offsite with our hash-tagged custom ThreadSol hoodies.

Goa was a lot of fun. We sang, drank, danced, chilled, laughed and celebrated a terrific year. An all-night-long disco visit capped the year 2015 and another six-hour-long bonfire on the beach made our bonds grow deeper.

No one could have anticipated that the fun and frolic of 2015 was drawing us towards a dark crevasse. Yes, it is true that a niche needs a visionary and no VC, and we had the support from a visionary but then, in the most uncertain choppy waters of the start-up life, even the most clairvoyant and clear-visioned can get blindsided.

The year 2016 was going to be a spectacular slow-motion crash that almost killed us.

Money in bank – winner, winner!
No champagne – it's burger dinner!

16

The Slow-Motion Crash of 2016

If you have ever seen an F1 race, you will know the pit stops are crucial for the race. The cars run at 320 kilometres per hour and they wear out their tires and deplete their fuel reserves. To replenish their fuel and get a fresh set of grippy tyres, the cars come into the pits where an elaborate and synchronized dance takes place. As soon as the car pulls to a stop, 12 people pounce on it. In a little over two seconds, these men change all four tyres of the car and the driver zooms out. When refuelling the cars, the pressurized fuel systems deliver an astonishing 12 litres of fuel per second! The fastest pit stop was carried out by the Red Bull racing team on Max Verstappen's car in the 2019 Brazilian GP. The pit crew changed four tires in 1.82 seconds!

This was never the norm. For almost 35 years, the pit stop was a super slow affair. The crew would labour to change the tires and put in fuel. Sometimes, the driver would get out of the car and help. At times he would nonchalantly stand by and smoke a cigarette and sign autographs. A pit stop could take as much as five minutes and it was broadly assumed that pitting a car was the end of the race for the team.

And then all of a sudden in 1981, the Brabham F1 team arrived at the races with a completely different outlook. They came with high torque wheel nut guns to remove old tires and install new ones in a matter of seconds. They also had a high-pressure fuel delivery system that refuelled the car in a matter of seconds and the car would leap back into the race in a jiffy. They set up a well-rehearsed and well-practised choreographed move to complete the pit stop at lightning speed. The pit crew also came with fireproof clothing and had a system of non-verbal gestures to speed up the processes. They must have looked completely out of place.

However, this gave a terrific tactical advantage to the Brabham F1 team. Their cars could run on lighter fuel loads that made them blazing fast, gaining 1.5–2 seconds per lap over their rivals and then, after 20 laps or so, they came back and got fresh fuel and fresh grippy tires. The pit stop cost 30 seconds or so but with a lighter, grippier car, they would wipe out the deficit with ease. The Brabham team was initially laughed at for their elaborate system, but very quickly everyone realized what a terrific game-changer this was.

Today, all pit stops in the F1 races follow (with even more improvements) what Brabham did in 1981. It showed two things. One, a well-planned, well-kitted and well-trained team always delivers an advantage. And two, those who look at the full picture can find areas of improvement better than those who write off certain aspects as something that cannot be improved.

On a cold January morning in 2016, when I came out of the meeting room, I felt the unmistakable whiff of the Brabham moment for ThreadSol. Every month's first Monday used to be a complete business review with all the founders and team heads. This would be a long 3–4-hour meeting where we would review the business and chart the path for the month and check our bearings with respect to the overall quarter and fiscal year performance targets for the business and also the individual departments. The results of this meeting would be then put into a deck and shared with the board of ThreadSol and all its investors.

After coming back from our fun-filled Goa trip, I had thrown a challenge to the team heads to think afresh about their division and find innovations that would deliver efficiency, speed and better results. We were to review all these in the monthly meeting of January 2016.

At the meeting were Jaya and Neeraj, who ran the project implementations and customer success for ThreadSol. Rohit, Srajan and Nikita Jain were the spearheads of this team and they put on a great show.

'What is the difference between these two photographs?' Rohit started the presentation with a split-screen image of the RoboCop (the Hollywood movie) with all its high-tech gadgetry and a pot-bellied Indian policeman with a feeble cane. The image elicited quite a laugh from the gathering.

'Both are law enforcement officers but as you can clearly see, the RoboCop image generates more reverence and awe. So, what is the moral?' He asked and paused to get some reactions.

After a few minutes of exchanges filled with levity, Rohit – in stark contrast to his hashtag #BestStories (for not delivering a climactic end to his storytelling) – delivered the message home.

'We at the ThreadSol project implementation team think that we could get a better response from the factory floor if we had an external image makeover. Let me present to you what we think we should look like . . .'

And in walked Nikita Jain and Srajan. They were dressed smartly in business attire – jacket and trousers – and were carrying a two-way radio transmitter in their belt buckles, a portable projector and printer, a laser pointer, a handheld laser distance measurement device and a sleek 11-inch MacBook. They looked a million bucks and a true RoboCop version of their radiant selves.

Everyone loved it. And with that, our implementation team went into a high-tech-look mode. The look exuded confidence and the gizmos accentuated the tech-savvy appeal that resulted in our consultants being more respected. In the next six months or so, the implementation days came down sharply by 33 per cent. That was a huge win – the team had thought through the problem and presented the solution brilliantly.

At the same meeting, Mausmi, Anshu and Shubham came up with a complete set of 100 key performance indicators (KPIs) to measure all the various departments' performance and we set about creating a pan ThreadSol business KPIs dashboard so that we could keep track of the individual departments and their progress in a clear transparent way.

This dashboard would be accessible to not only the founders but the various team heads and some other important members so that a group of 20-odd people could keep a regular eye on the daily KPI-based performance of the business. This democratization of data and scientific rigour in gauging the performance of all the divisions through 100 KPIs would become the cornerstone of all our organizational improvements for years to come. Thanks to the 100-odd KPIs that Mausmi had baked into the business, I was always in touch with the macro business indicators in real time and so were the other ThreadSol business leaders. Therefore, calls and discussions were mostly super swift and it made us work faster and leaner. I hated doing long meetings in person or worse – over the Internet! Except for a weekly Monday 8 p.m. sales catch-up, I had no recurring scheduled meetings. It meant that I could travel furiously and catch up with the team in India on important issues without holding anyone back.

The KPIs also had another effect. No one could predict that this super rigour on data-driven business management would one day generate early warnings of impending doom and would also serve to be the north star in guiding us out of the doldrums.

As we expected the Series A raised $3 million to hit our bank account soon, we decided to accelerate our hiring process with a mandate to swell to a size of 140 people in the next six months from our current strength of 50. We also finalized the lease for our new office. It would be a block away from our small office and the new facility would be able to seat the expanded team and would have four floors and a basement where we would set up recreational facilities. We also decided to take up a proper office space in Kolkata and hire more folks there.

When I came out of the meeting room that January morning in 2016, it seemed we were on course to scale the business with the cash that was about to hit the bank. And a few weeks later when I stood in the new sparkling ThreadSol office and spoke to CBNC's *Young Turks*, I reiterated that even though apparel tech was not a thing for most VCs, we should be looked at as a worldwide category creator for this space.

Two calls arrived on the day CNBC aired its show on ThreadSol. I got a call to participate in the Government of India's Make in India mega-fair in Mumbai as one of the four Indian start-ups that were chosen to be showcased. The other one delighted me even more – an invitation to do a TEDx talk in the mill city of Bhilwara. Looked like our little gig was being noticed in the big town!

Both events were fantastic. The Make in India event in Mumbai was held at the BKC fairground and it was transformed into a glittering LCD-infested hi-tech paradise. The prime minister inaugurated the event. I had a seven-minute live TV presentation in front of a 5,000-strong audience, followed by a 30-minute live TV panel discussion with three other brilliant start-up founders.

The TEDx talk was also a lot of fun. It was a great feeling to stand on the famed red circular carpet of TED and deliver my talk. When I spoke from the dais, I could see Mausmi, Abhishek and Bratish – my long-term fierce friends and co-founders sitting in the audience. It was a victory for all of us. Just after the TED talk, Mausmi won the prestigious CNBC Woman Entrepreneur of the Year award. She was presented with the award at a glamorous event in New Delhi.

Had I changed as ThreadSol began to scale its heights? On the personal front, I had become a very private person. Gone were the days when I would write a blog every now and then. My cycling was also gone – mostly because of my crazy travel schedule. I used to follow football, F1, world rally car, tennis, cricket and chess as an avid fan of all these sports. Now, all I could do was catch a few highlights or just read up on the scores over the weekends. Weekends were off but I never switched off from work. One reason for that was Bangladesh, which worked Saturdays and Sundays, and many a times I would dash off to Dhaka to do televised interviews with the apparel industry experts, minister of commerce, etc. for a weekend of marketing work. I have no idea how Wilson and Nikita and the marketing team got us these breaks – but they kept us firmly in the limelight and kept me perennially standing in immigration queues. I was always on the move.

Entrepreneurship is an almost infinite strategy game with infinite possible moves and infinite inputs. The volume of everyday drama is so high that it seems like being on an addictive drug that keeps the patrons going and wanting more. And it is seductive to give in to the pace, give in to the constant overload of the latest updates and give in to the temptation of jumping into everything. The four of us realized that we needed to find regular downtimes from this crazy whirlwind of a deluge of activities that would take up every square inch of the very fabric of the present time.

Abhishek would take his downtime and compose his poetry. In

the middle of running a start-up, he actually published a collection of his poems, and it was well received. Abhishek also created a literary society in ThreadSol where budding poets, writers, stand-up artists, etc. would perform once every fortnight. Bratish went deep into his photography and formed a photography society in ThreadSol. They would routinely do photo walks and have photography competitions. Mausmi went deep into reading and also wrote many books for the apparel industry and built a highly popular video blog. She also was part of the ThreadSol dance troupe and they performed routinely and were extremely popular internally.

And I formed an in-house rock band. We called it Dhaage, thread in Hindi. I had no skills in playing the drums but looking at the available talents in ThreadSol, I thought it was worth a shot. I bought a drum kit purely out of whim and taught myself drumming. I had learnt Indian classical music as a kid for five years and that learning came good after almost two decades. I gave 90 minutes to my drumming each day for six months and I improved swiftly on my drum skills and before long was proficient enough to start playing. It added a fantastic dimension to my life.

And I would play long hours of table tennis with the folks. I had been a decent player in my school and college days, and in a corporate tournament of 128, I was once the runner-up 12 years back. But now at almost 40, I found it hard to keep up with the 25-year-olds of ThreadSol. So, I became a thinking player who would study the young opponents, discover their flaws and change my game to exploit those weaknesses to win the games. Sometimes, I would let the fast platers blow themselves up early in the game and then slyly come back and register a sneaky win. I was amazed at the number of ways I discovered to win despite not being the fastest owing to my age. There were regular tournaments that were attended by the whole organization with fervent support and that added to the fun quotient at the workplace. I also did a paragliding course. I had been afraid of heights and the only way to conquer that was to face the fear square on. Jumping from a 300-foot cliff with the glider glued to my back was scary but liberating. When you face fears and want to trounce that – that's when magic happens.

90!

I gazed at my WhatsApp in disbelief. It was May 2016. I was at the Kuala Lumpur airport making my way to Jakarta and the overnight cheap flight from Delhi had made me groggy and tired.

The year 2016 had started in very high gear for us. It looked like all was going great. The Brabham F1 team had made its point yet again, this time in ThreadSol's avatar. Five months later, we had only 90 days to live. How could this be possible? We were growing rapidly. Business was good. We were hiring rapidly, and we now had a team of 130 people. We had opened our HQ in Singapore and two new regional offices in Ho Chi Minh City in Vietnam and another in Jakarta in Indonesia. We had salespeople in India, Sri Lanka, Vietnam, Indonesia, China and Bangladesh. We had two great products – IntelloCut and IntelloBuy. How could we have again come to a point where we had 90 days of cash left in the bank?

As I was thinking about all of this, my phone rang again. It was a group call with all the founders, initiated by Mausmi.

'Hey, guys. What's going on?' I said.

'I mean, I don't know . . . How are we again at this life and death juncture?' Abhishek was clearly not happy. You can make out that he is not happy when he goes ballistic with the overuse of the phrase 'I mean, I don't know . . .'

'Yes, let me explain.' Mausmi was super calm. 'The DD of the Series A investment has been going on for the last five months. E&Y's DD team is saying it could take another two months before they submit the report. Meanwhile, we have paid for all the expenses of HQ creation in Singapore, regional office creation in Indonesia and Vietnam, marketing spends, salary load of 130 people. We have done all of this from our profits.

We did this because our investors gave us the full green light to aggressively expand. We followed their dictum. The DD report was to be delivered in January 2016 and now we are sitting in May. All these have drained our resources. Now we need to get the investment money. The KPIs we had set up in January are giving us an early warning that we will be short of cash by August 2016.'

We all fell silent.

'Why is the DD taking so long?' Bratish asked.

'The E&Y team is very slow and fastidious and as we kept on adding offices in Indonesia and Vietnam, the scope of work increased,' Mausmi explained.

'So, what are we going to do?' I asked.

'I have cancelled all marketing spends until the money comes in. All recruitment is also frozen. We are into severe cost-cutting measures while I, Shubham and Sameer work closely with E&Y and the investors to complete the DD and get the money in the bank.'

'This is highly suboptimal. Stopping all these growth-related expenses will have a negative effect. This is just stupid,' I said. But I knew we had no choice but to do as Mausmi had suggested.

And with that 2016 turned on its head. From going guns blazing in the first few months, we were forced to take an extremely conservative fiscal approach. All spending was put on the back burner. As a result, our marketing came to a grinding halt and that immediately affected the sales expansions. Every morning I woke up with a new number on the countdown clock. Days stretched into weeks and weeks into months, and the situation remained grim. It was hard to explain to the team why we were applying brakes to a machine that was moving so well.

The investors sympathized with our situation and we had many calls with the E&Y team, but we hit a major corporate wall. We were now talking to E&Y India, Singapore, Vietnam and Indonesia, and the complicated coordination and corporate bureaucracy swallowed ThreadSol right up.

The loss of time and stringent control of the budget hurt us badly. The pace is the most important winning chip in the hands of a start-up and a loss of pace makes a lot of things hard. It slows down the growth, and just the loss of a month can add the asking rates for the subsequent months to become so great that the targets that looked challenging but achievable at the beginning of the year suddenly start to look insurmountable. Add to that the extra pressure of fiscal rigidity and you have the perfect storm.

Typically, our marketing and sales team would identify the potential customers first. Then the marketing team would work hard to reach out to the owners and CXOs of the business through various channels. The sales team would land and do demos and trial runs. Finally, the marketing team would put up a glitzy apparel tech symposium where we would invite all the prospects and impress them with our super-slick event and super-inspiring content. Also, the marketing team would get us media and PR mentions and regular television interviews with industry stalwarts in various countries. With not enough money to spare, all these activities were retarded and had a significant impact on our topline growth.

Full marks to our team for trying to accelerate with no gas in the tank though. The marketing team found creative ways to reach out to people and started a strong video vlog and a vibrant blog to attract more people. These platforms gained a fair amount of popularity and we received many inbound requests that offset the lack of marketing dollars.

The sales team also dug in. Everyone went back to the style of the early days to work on a few accounts and nurture them with care. Ankit, in Indonesia, made some creative decisions and decided to go to the large manufacturing plants without appointments to see if people would meet him. Many times, he was shooed away from the gates and he would befriend the guards and coax them to share the number of the directors and somehow this crazy process worked. He was not just able to crack meetings but also close deals. Great effort!

The project implementation teams went beyond their remit and at every implementation, they took up extra work to convince the factory management to expand to the other units. The tech team delivered an entire Artificial Intelligence-driven module to add to the ease and save more fabric and get more ROI for our solutions.

Everyone chipped in and we all clenched our teeth through the dollar drought. As months passed, the business started to move better and we learnt how to run a lean ship. But we paid a price for this as the business came down from its steep growth of over 100 per cent to a more moderate 40 per cent growth trajectory. The democratization of the data and KPIs helped everyone in the senior team understand the situation and make sacrifices for the sake of the greater good.

Every morning we all kept a lookout on the number of days to live and took a deep breath and went about our business. We all knew that the drought would end one day. It was a matter of time. I always thought that Catamaran could have done better by putting pressure on E&Y to complete the DD faster. However, they left us in the open to deal with E&Y and we got massively delayed.

42!

As I woke up in my hotel room in Singapore, I felt a gush of rage. It was November 2016 – almost 11 months since the DD began – and here we were with no visible end to this agony. The business was running on fumes and though the team had shown exemplary tenacity, it was stupid to hold off an engine from leaping forward and driving it conservatively when we could go much faster.

I shot off a strongly worded email to E&Y and then another to Catamaran. Without the growth capital, we had to leave a lot of things undone and if they could not get us the capital, we would have to reconsider our joint future.

Within an hour, I got a call from Rounak from Catamaran. I told him that he needed to chasten E&Y. The call was ill-tempered. Rounak was not impressed with me but I couldn't care less. This was not personal. Rounak promised that he would get things moving soon and that I should not worry.

After the call, as I stood on the hotel balcony and watched the Clark Quay riverside markets open, I felt my heart descend to the stomach.

What if Catamaran backs out? We have 42 days of money in the bank. How will we survive? There is no way I can find another investor in 42 days. Will Blume help me by giving me a bridge round immediately?

I texted Ashish that I needed to speak to him urgently. I saw two blue ticks in front of the message. He had seen the message. However, he didn't reply.

Is he busy? Is he ignoring me? Catamaran is an investor in Blume as well. Did I piss off both of them in one go?

I had too many negative thoughts in my mind. So, I went and woke Mausmi up. We had reached the hotel at 4 a.m. and she had barely slept five hours. She calmed me down and I felt better.

We were in Singapore to get our employment passes and work permits. The process was smooth and very impressive. Singapore is a study of efficiency and everything moves like clockwork. The cleanliness of Singapore is unparalleled. Except for Scandinavian countries, I have not seen such a level of cleanliness anywhere. There were strict rules and severely punitive fines to beat the residents and visitors to adhere to the rules. The public transport was fantastic. Every building had a six-digit code and if you typed just that on Google Maps, you would reach the destination without the added hassles of writing the building name, street number, blah-blah. The only downside – Singapore was expensive as hell!

We spent the afternoon in the employment office getting registered, getting our passes and opening bank accounts, etc. It was 4 p.m. when we completed everything, and we came back to the hotel to take a nap. I fell into deep sleep as soon as I hit the bed. The red-eye flight, the early morning hustle and the errands of the day had made me tired.

I heard Mausmi's phone ring and I heard her pick up the call. I drifted into sleep again. Minutes later she was shaking me awake. 'Manasij, wake up . . . wake up . . .'

'What the hell is wrong with you?' I was still sleepy.

'Manasij, the DD report is here. Catamaran has credited $2.5 million to us.' Mausmi was excited. She was jumping up and down.

I woke up thunderstruck.

Wow. After 11 months of wait, the money is finally in. I sat up on the bed and thought.

'This is incredible. We must go and celebrate,' Mausmi said.

'Yes, let's go. Let's have dinner at the riverside and enjoy the evening,' I said as we hugged and kissed.

We conveyed the good news to Abhishek and Bratish and then to the team heads and all the folks at ThreadSol. Everyone was relieved. There were some celebrations and some high-fives, but mostly it was an expression of relief.

'Congratulations. Finally, it is in. Hope we will have some money to kick-start the marketing again. We have lost a lot of ground and it will take time to regain it. Hope you guys are not looking for a miraculous bounce back in no time.' Wilson sent his congratulatory message with a tone of caution.

'Need to hire folks in China. Please approve it now. It will take a good six to eight months before we find a good guy and make him worthy of pulling his weight in sales.' Kundan sent his demands from China.

Similar messages flooded our inboxes as Mausmi and I got ready to go to our riverside dinner. I had my mind set on crabs and I told her that I intended to enjoy this hard-fought investor money.

I wondered, if I had taken this strong stance before, would Catamaran have been more active and put more pressure on E&Y? Was it my fault that I hadn't pushed hard enough early on? Mausmi and I both talked about this as we walked through the Friday evening festivities of the famed Clark Quay riverside, while checking out the restaurants.

'$200 for a crab dinner? Are these guys crazy?' I fumed.

'I could get a similar-sized crab in Sri Lanka for $20.'

Mausmi laughed. 'Does this look like Colombo to you?'

After an hour's search for 'decently prized crabs', we had nothing. It seemed like the timely investment, a decent crab meal was about to elude us.

'See you want a riverside dinner, don't you?' she asked.

'Yes, I do,' I said.

'Okay, you stand here for five minutes, I will solve this for you.' She left me standing at the riverside. I watched her walk away and turn a corner.

It was a new moon night, and the Friday fever had gripped the riverside, which was teeming with people and restaurants.

I felt a tap on my shoulder and turned around. Mausmi was standing with two large brown bags.

'Here is your McChicken with extra cheese and fries with Piri Piri sauce – just the way you love and your large strawberry shake and the same for me as well.' She extended her right hand to pass one bag to me.

'You know how much this cost? $20! This is our riverside dinner. Now, let's sit right at the water's edge and eat our dinner.'

I laughed. A McDonald's dinner for getting a Series A investment!

'Shouldn't we have splurged a bit?' I said. 'After all, we got our investment today.'

'Didn't you try hard enough looking through 20-odd restaurants? Now, let's just sit and enjoy our riverside dinner. Splurging is not important. Enjoying the moment is more important.'

She looked at me and said, 'This is who we are.'

Part III

Let's Sell This . . .

More innovation . . .

Will buy you, will buy you not . . .

No money for originality . . .

Acquisition saga . . .

Endgame . . .

17

This Place Is Funny

2016 was a dead year. Yet we managed to make some gains. Pakistan, Bangladesh, Sri Lanka, Cambodia, Vietnam, Myanmar, Kenya, Ethiopia, Egypt, China, Thailand, Malaysia, Indonesia, Philippines, Jordan, Bahrain, Fiji, Turkey, Mexico . . .

By 2016, our emissaries had planted the ThreadSol flag in all these countries and we were a truly international business. Initially, some of the idiosyncrasies and peculiarities of these places used to stump us but then we all learnt that the world is indeed a funny place. It is way easy to do business in Western countries where things are predictable and the law of the land is firmly established.

It was almost midnight when the doorbell rang. Kundan was buried deep under the layers of quilts and was fast asleep. In the adjacent bed, Wilson was still awake and was browsing the Internet and keeping abreast with the sports updates that he religiously followed. The bell rang again.

'This is stupid. We didn't ask for anything. Why is anyone ringing the bell?' Wilson thought. He got up and opened the door.

To his immense surprise, there were three policemen, the hotel manager and some other folks at the door.

'Kon ve caum een?' The policeman with the most stars on his chest asked in a thick North African accent. Weirdly, he was wearing badass aviator shades at this hour of the night.

'Yes, you can come in.' Wilson showed them in.

The party came in and occupied the chairs and the beds. The senior policeman settled in the biggest sofa and gestured something to the other two and they leapt into the suitcases, cupboards and whatever belongings that Wilson and Kundan had in the room. The commotion made Kundan snap out of his slumber and he sat up dazed as the two policemen ravaged all their belongings.

'What is this about?' Wilson asked.

'Don't speak.' The senior policeman said in a menacing tone.

Wilson and Kundan watched the police turn the room upside down. After they had wreaked enough havoc, the two policemen said something to their senior and he gestured for them to go out. Then he rose from the sofa, pulled his aviator shades down and looked at Wilson and Kundan, slid his shades up again and walked out, leaving Wilson and Kundan in utter bewilderment.

'Sir, this is Adis Ababa.' The hotel manager spoke finally. 'In Ethiopian culture, we don't appreciate gays.' He continued his lecture to the two utterly amazed hotel guests. 'The police suspect that you guys are gays. Otherwise, why would you two gentlemen share one room?'

Wilson and Kundan finally understood the problem. They were in Ethiopia for ThreadSol business and were in Adis Ababa for two days. They had taken a hotel near the airport so that it would be easier for them to move. To cut costs, they were sharing a room.

'We no allow gays in this hotel. Plus, you have long hairs. Men no have long hair in Ethiopia. Only gays have long hairs.' The manager pointed to Wilson and delivered the verdict.

Twenty minutes later, Wilson and Kundan were thrown out of the hotel. It was way past midnight and the two couldn't believe the turn of events.

Wilson called Mausmi.

'Hey Mausmi, guess what? We got kicked out of the hotel. This place is funny.'

~

'Last price $70,000,' Anas said.

'No, I want $60,000.'

'No, sir, I can't do $60,000. My last price is $70,000.'

'You can. You should try.'

'No, I really can't,' Anas put his foot down.

'Plus, we are getting late. We have to get to the airport and our flight is in one hour,' Prateek, from Anas's sale team added. The negotiation had been going on for the last 90 minutes with a big-shot owner of a hugely influential Bangladesh factory.

'Look Mr Anas, I like you and your software,' said the big burly brute sitting in his resplendent office, smoking his pipe like a chimney. 'But I do not like your price. I am telling you $60,000 is very good.'

'No, sir, I really cannot,' Anas said, 'It has to be $70,000.'

The brute had deep folds on his forehead.

'You know who I am?'

'Everyone gives me the price I want. I am very powerful and very connected. You see this factory? Do you know what is underneath this factory?' he asked.

Anas and Prateek didn't answer. They just stared at the burly brute intently.

'Underneath are dead bodies.' The brute said with the air of a megalomaniac dictator. 'No one can find them again. I always get what I want. No police, no army, nothing can touch me and my business. You understand?' he said. 'What was the price again?'

'$70,000,' said Anas. He was shaken and so was Prateek. They had dealt with plenty of threats but no one had ever issued such a direct one.

The room became quiet. The brute was looking at Prateek and his silent gaze felt more ominous by the second.

'Okay. I like your persistence. You win,' he said.

Then he pressed a bell and a meek-looking tie- and jacket-clad guy walked in.

'Yes, MD Sir, you called me?' he said.

'Yes, issue a purchase order for IntelloBuy software from ThreadSol immediately and I will sign and they will countersign,' the brute said while he bellowed a big cloud of smoke.

'What would be the amount?' the meek guy asked.

'$65,000,' the brute said and then he turned towards Prateek and Anas and said, 'Okay, right?'

'Yes. Okay,' Anas said.

The PO came and the brute signed. Anas countersigned. The deal was done.

'One small problem,' Prateek said. 'We will miss our flight. It leaves in 30 minutes. We can't make it.'

'No, you will make it.' The brute was smiling. He pointed his finger to the meek guy and said, 'Get the bird ready and get me the civil aviation secretary on the phone.'

Thirty minutes later, the passengers of the Kolkata-bound Bimaan Bangladesh flight saw a helicopter land just near the plane and two young men in debonair jackets and ties jump out and walk into the flight that had been waiting for the last 20 minutes. They were mighty confused when the two guys sat in the economy class though – they had assumed the two guys must be tycoons.

Anas called me from his mobile as the plane was taxiing. 'Hey Manasij, you won't believe what just happened. This place is funny.'

Kundan was hungry.

He had endured a red-eye from Delhi to Shanghai and right after landing, he had gone to the biggest Adidas factory in the region for a deal. One reason we put Kundan in charge of China – the biggest apparel manufacturing destination in the world – was because he could eat anything.

I have spent an evening with him in the Beijing night market, where you can sink your teeth into a stick of fried scorpions, grilled tarantula spiders, live octopus (you eat that with a hot sauce), fried earthworm, diced and smoked snake or even drink duck blood. Kundan was at ease with all kinds of animal protein and if it swam, ran, squatted in mud, crawled, slithered or flew – he would eat that animal without complaints. But give him a bowl of cabbage soup and he will be sick for three days. We joked, 'Dude you were born to be in China.'

He was also hungry for success. While Anas was handling Bangladesh and Saurav was handling Southeast Asia, Kundan wanted a big ticket geography under his belt. We always wanted to set up an outpost in China but had always been stumped by this vast country. China was a salty place to set up business on a shoestring. If you went to China on a holiday and stayed at a five-star place surrounded by English speakers, you would sail. Try doing cheap hotels, local taxis and local transport and you realize that without Mandarin, you are just paralysed. Plus, China is expensive. Marketing, wages, living costs were five times more than in Delhi or Mumbai. And an average Chinese thinks of India like an average Indian thinks of Pakistan – a poor neighbour you are way superior to in all aspects, although there is none of the open hatred that India and Pakistan seem to share.

Our China dreams took off in 2016 when Abhishek accidentally met Siddharth (Sid, as we called him) on a badminton court. Sid was a Punjabi kid who had studied in China for years, spoke fluent Mandarin, had a Chinese girlfriend and was itching to find a job and a way back to Shanghai. We were a natural fit. Kundan was paired with him and they ran China for us.

Previously, we had had a policy of going to China by not going to China. As Saurav would close deals all over Southeast Asia – invariably he would find sister businesses of our customers in Vietnam, Taiwan, the Philippines and Indonesia in China. So, we had a trickle-down revenue from China anyway. And Chinese factories were behemoths – ten to hundred times larger than a factory in India. They were super advanced and super technical. Yet, we kept winning them. Kundan had to do all sorts of somersaults to manage these wins in China with his zero Mandarin in the early days. He once jammed with a bass guitarist manager of a large group to win him over. Luckily, Kundan was the lead singer of our rock band; so the jamming must have been good for us to win the deals. But we never had a native speaker who could run the country. The moment Sid arrived, Kundan packed his bags and did not return for almost three years.

So, after closing the deal with the largest Adidas vendor in the region (Luenthai group – who owned a huge shipping corporation and the brand Sketchers), Kundan started dreaming of food. He could not endure another 90 minutes of car ride to get back to the city and wanted to find something to eat.

And right outside the factory gate was the answer to his

prayers. On a wooden hard-cart, he could see steaming dumplings. So, while Sid was booking a cab, Kundan ventured towards the street vendor and decided to take matters into his hand.

'I want momo,' he told the big burly Chinese guy who had tattoos all over his arms and had long hair curled up in a bun over his head. He looked perplexed.

Kundan repeated, 'Momo, momo, you understand?' he said.

The big guy looked pissed. So Kundan tried one last time. He put his index finger on his lips pointing to his mouth, 'Momo, momo, momo . . .'

The big guy was staring at him menacingly. Sid had caught the last part of the interaction and he immediately whisked Kundan into the taxi.

'Dude, what the hell were you doing?' Sid asked.

'I was asking for momo,' Kundan replied. 'What was wrong with that?'

'I mean you pointed to your mouth and asked that six-footer hunk of a rock for momo?' Sid asked.

'Yes. Why?' Kundan was still grabbing at the straws.

Sid burst out laughing. He called Mausmi on his WeChat.

'Mausmi, you won't believe what just happened. Kundan just asked a six-foot-tall tattooed muscular Chinese hunk for momo, which in Mandarin means to make affectionate love.'

'God damn it,' Kundan fumed in his car seat, 'This place is funny.'

The lessons we learnt through these adventures? The apparel industry is a labour-intensive industry and you have to work in countries that may not be on anyone's travel bucket list. Over the years, we learnt that all the management principles, the lofty best practices, the gold-plated playbooks, none of these seem to work in these banana republics and you needed to find fresh inspirations and develop grit and determination to survive and build and scale.

However, what we didn't know at the time was that very soon ThreadSol would end up expanding to the Western developed world as well.

The scope of our innovation was about to take another leap and this time we were to taste the Wild Wild West and the Wild Wild East!

18

Wild Wild West and Wild Wild East!

A Coruña, Spain. September 2016.

It was a rainy day. Jaya stood by the wall and contemplated the scene in front of her. A wave of anxiety was washing over her. In the next eight hours, she would know if the newest innovation of ThreadSol was going to deliver value. There were 60 mammoth-sized denim rolls in front of her. The floor was empty with no operators and only mechanical robots.

'Rain, rain go to Spain, Come again another day . . .' She remembered the nursery rhyme and then chuckled, 'But I am in Spain . . .'

Cut to Noida, India

It was a rainy day there too. The rain was falling relentlessly on the large glass walls of the ThreadSol office boardroom. Mausmi stood by the wall and contemplated the scene in front of her. A wave of anxiety was washing over her. In the next eight hours, she would know if the newest innovation of ThreadSol was going to deliver value. There were 60 miniature-sized denim rolls in front of her. The boardroom was full of ThreadSol leadership team members – all anxiously waiting to hear from her.

Cut to A Coruña, Spain

Jaya saw the automatic robotic system pick up a random denim roll from the tray and start laying that on the super-large table. She noted the roll number and sent a WhatsApp to Mausmi.

Cut to Noida, India

'People, the robots have picked up roll no 23.'

A frenzy whipped through the room. Silky went to the corner of the table and picked up a roll of kitchen towel that had 'number 23' written over it. And just as the robot in A Coruña had spread the fabric on the table, Silky too spread it on the boardroom table.

The two tables, 7,500 kilometres apart, were playing out the same scenario in parallel. Meanwhile, a dozen engineers in Noida went through the software logs to see if everything was running fine. I was sitting in the glass-covered planning room where the Zara folks were busy putting their tally marks on their cutting cards. Next to me lay my laptop that ran our Artificial Intelligence software!

Let's flashback. . .

A month back Jaya and I visited A Coruña, where we were invited by the fashion giant Zara. I was blown away by the factory compound. There were six factories of titanic proportions, all connected underground by a 10 kilometres long automatic cable and pulley system that ran garments, fabric rolls, cut panels and accessories from one place to another.

The fabric store was as large as a cathedral and the cutting rooms were as big as football fields. There were only a few people around. Most of the stuff was automated. The only thing that was manual was the planning. The two-person planning team had a card where they put tally marks on the number of rolls laid and cut on the table with automated machines. Right in the middle of a sea of automation, it stuck out as a sore archaic system.

Looking at the setup, I realized that our system would need significant tweaks to work in an all-automated environment. The Zara people gave us 28 days for a second chance, and I went back and rewrote the algorithms with the folks back in India. In a frenzied development spree, Abhishek, Bratish and the folks rallied and delivered the software.

Okay, now back to the present . . .

Jaya and I came back to A Coruña in Spain a month later. Our freshly written software was still under testing and the glitches were not completely ironed out. Zara gave us a huge order with 60 fabric rolls of denim to work with. As I was talking to the floor in charge, I saw Jaya slip out and go to the fabric bay. To my amazement, she started photographing the fabric rolls and I kept the floor in charge engaged.

'What are you going to do with the pics?' I asked her on our way back to the hotel.

'Have you seen the movie *The Martian*?' she asked.

'Yes, I have. What about *The Martian*?'

'You see, when Matt Damon gets stuck on Mars, he goes and digs up the Pathfinder. The NASA folks also restart the Pathfinder model in the Jet Propulsion Laboratory – JPL. And with that, whatever Matt Damon does on the planet Mars with the Pathfinder, the JPL folks do the same with their replica. And they communicate. Do you understand?' she said.

'These pics are your Pathfinder?' I was flummoxed.

'I will send these pics to Noida. The folks can get scale-model dummy rolls made with kitchen towels. So, a 100-metre roll would become a 100-centimetre kitchen towel roll, and they can replicate whatever happens here on their table tops in the office, and if any glitch shows up, they can immediately calibrate the system by looking at the physical kitchen towel rolls. Now, do you see?' She was smiling.

I was impressed. Start-ups make people creative and hungry for success. Here we were, on the world stage – given to us by the biggest fashion brand on the planet. It doesn't always get bigger than this and the ingenuity of ThreadSol was on display.

Jaya was running the cutting floor at A Coruña and Silky was running the replica in the Noida office as everyone watched the software perform flawlessly and at the end of the execution, save two enormous denim rolls – a huge victory for our innovation. Again!

The jaws of the Zara folks were so wide open you could have sailed a Panamax cargo ship, carrying all of Zara collections, right through it.

We celebrated with some exquisite Galician food that evening, dining on the best octopus I have ever had (they call it Pulpo) and some terrific Iberian Ham (they call it el Jamon) and some authentic Sangria.

Two days later, the pride of the largest jacket factory in Porto, Portugal, fell to the might of our new innovation. A month later Neeraj would tame the largest suiting factory in Serbia with the same sword. At the same time, Kundan would take down a mammoth factory in China. Saurav would make a super-large

Nicaraguan unit eat humble pie. Ankit would score a win in Fiji. The latest innovation worked better than the old one and was super easy and super slick!

Triumphant, I came back to Zara in October 2016 to complete the deal. I had planned on feasting on some more pulpo and el-jamon with a signed deal. But then there were deeper lessons for us in the Wild Wild West!

Zara said no. Our months of hard work had turned up a naught. It was highly disappointing. Unlike our other customers, Zara was a brand. They didn't want to save the fabric that they had already negotiated and the factories had already bought. It was no use to them. So, even though we could save them fabric, it was not valuable for them. What was valuable for them was to do this before they bought – at the time of negotiations. Basically, they said that they loved the results, but they wanted us to put our technology a little ahead in the supply chain – at a time when they negotiate with their vendors for the garment cost (where fabric is often 50–70 per cent of the total cost). If we could create a product that helped them to reduce the cost of the garment at the costing stage – that would be valuable.

It was a great insight. Till now, we were working with the manufacturers where our tech always sailed. If we could repackage the solution, we could work with the world's biggest brands in the US and Europe. So, even though Zara didn't buy, they showed us where we could innovate next – where we could get the next pot of gold. I remember Zara as a victory in defeat – but a defeat nonetheless!

Entrepreneurship is all about finding opportunities in debacles and we did exactly that.

Shangri-La Hotel, Hong Kong. November 2016.

The main ballroom had 12 large round tables. The neat dais had a podium and two large projector screens. Nikita and Wilson were busily walking in and out of the room to look after the final arrangements. The photographers and the video team were doing a final round of equipment checks. As one of the sound technicians was arming me with the collar mike, I looked around.

Here are the Asia MD of Under Armour, Brooks Brothers, Carrefour, Kiabi, Tchibo and JCPenney. And the directors of Gap, H&M, PVH, Adidas, Nike, Lululemon, Target and Helly Hansen and Li & Fung – all international brands gathered under one roof to listen to our story. I was impressed looking at the turnout and quality of the audience. Our marketing team had done a lot of work to get the heavyweights of the industry to come to the event.

'Gentlemen, ladies,' I began my presentation, 'thank you for coming. We are from ThreadSol. Before we get into the contents of today's presentation, let me share a funny story from 1968 concerning Dr Spencer Silver. He was a scientist working hard to create the world's strongest adhesive for the company 3M in the US. Well, he failed.

'Unfortunately for Dr Spencer, he ended up inventing the weakest adhesive of all times. But his weak glue had one interesting characteristic – you could stick this multiple times. And that led to the creation of Post-it notes, the omnipresent coloured glue pads in every office that you can stick anywhere and remove and restick somewhere else. So, Dr Spencer found spectacular success in his spectacular failure.

'When I went to Zara in A Coruña, Spain, I wanted to sell them our flagship product – IntelloCut – that would help them save fabric. We did a very high-pressure trial and showed them very good savings.' I showed the picture of the two gargantuan denim rolls that we had saved in the Zara factory.

'But the Zara folks threw me a curved ball. They told me that they had no interest in saving fabric. They wanted to reduce their fabric consumption at the stage when they finalize costing with the manufacturers. They also wanted something that they could use to automate the costing process and negotiate effectively with manufacturers worldwide. So, we were defeated in our quest in Spain.' I stopped and gazed at the audience.

'But, just like Dr Spencer, we found that we can build a solution that can find the most accurate and scientific costs of any garment using Artificial Intelligence and then going further, we crafted a solution that can negotiate with your manufacturers on cost, just like you do today manually on emails – except our solution's AI bot will complete the negotiations with the manufacturers. So, you can cost accurately, save cost and save time. And that is, ladies and gentlemen, the third innovation from the stables of ThreadSol. And it is called Intello3C!'

Then I went along to demo our AI-powered fashion brand costing and negotiation tool – the Intello3C! By the time the symposium ended, we had signed up for trials with most of the major brands.

We were now a business with three products. Whilst IntelloCut and IntelloBuy delivered fantastic fabric savings for apparel manufacturers, the latest innovation Intello3C provided international fashion brands with the opportunity to automate their garment costing and negotiation process with our AI solution.

The snub that I had gotten in the Wild Wild West of A Coruña, at Zara's hands, was well forgotten and within months, we had posted spectacular saving results in many large Western apparel brands. All the trials happened in Hong Kong, Shanghai,

Shenzhen, Jakarta, Bangkok, Ho Chi Minh City, Dhaka, etc. – all over the Wild Wild East!

~

Jakarta, Indonesia. December 2016.

It was my fifth trip to the capital city of the world's fourth most populous country – Indonesia.

When Ankit and I reached the Four Seasons, Jakarta, I was half dead from a four-hour drive from Bandung, 200 kilometres from Jakarta, and also relieved that it was the last meeting of the trip and that I was getting on a plane in six hours to go back home. I looked at the meeting invite and it read 'David John Berry, GSD, Coats'. This was set up by Nikita. The meeting notes were cryptic or probably my brain was a mush from the long car ride. It said, 'We had a good word with him in an event in Dhaka. He wants to meet you to see how we can work with GSD.'

I knew GSD was a 40-year-old British company and they had collated the apparel industry's sewing data, which they had developed with International Labour Organization. All the major apparel brands worldwide used their technology for benchmarking the sewing cost of the apparels. They were acquired by Coats PLC, a $1.5 billion UK company, which was the world leader in thread manufacture.

I was expecting to see a stiff upper-lipped Brit in crisp formal clothing and in walked David, wearing a traditional Indonesian batik print beach shirt and cargo shorts with stylish sunglasses. The first thing he said was, 'Call me Dave.'

He was a boisterous fella in his early 50s, 6-foot tall and of medium build, who cracked jokes at will and laughed heartily. We hit it off really well and shared a beer and exchanged notes on the apparel industry.

'So, have you tried to work with Coats ever?' he asked.

'Well, two years ago, when we had just two or three customers, I met the Coats CEO Paul Foreman in Sri Lanka at an event,' I said.

'Well, Paul is gone. But he has set up a software business in Coats. It is called Coats Global Services. GSD was acquired by this entity.' We clanged our bottles for the third round of beer and Dave said, 'We are meeting in Bangkok in January 2017. I will see if you could come to do a quick demonstration of your products. I have heard good things about you guys from many of my customers.'

Unknowingly, Dave had set the wheels in motion for the most important step of our start-up life.

Goa. December end, 2016.

Our yearly ritual of going to Goa at the end of a year with the whole team continued. The three days in the North Goa resort with sun and sand was a welcome break. It was great fun to see the young and energetic team make the most of the annual break.

In 2016, we had grown by just 43 per cent – a far cry from our 300 per cent plus growth the year before. It was like batting the whole day on a broken cricket pitch and scoring a dour 50 after scoring a breezy 50-ball century in the previous inning. We were clocking $1.8 million (₹14.1 crore) in revenue – well below the expected $2.5 million for the year – thanks to pulling back on marketing and sales spends owing to a cash crunch. Considering the fact that we had survived through a year-long funding winter and had 42 days of money left in the tank, this was not at all a bad performance. However, Mausmi, Abhishek, Bratish and I knew that this argument would be taken kindly by the existing investors who had seen the struggle up close and personal themselves, but it would not bode well with the future investors who want to see dizzying growth every year. Any time a dip occurs, that's a blemish on your record, and that makes fundraising harder.

In my books, 2016 was a lost opportunity – a slow-motion crash! If we had received the Series A funding in time, we could have really made an impact. This late fund infusion meant a wasted opportunity for 2016 and that would have a knock-on effect in 2017 as well. It takes time to deploy the funds and then reap the rewards from it. Since we received the Series A funding of $3 million almost in November 2016, the first half of 2017 would go into deploying the fund and one could expect to see the results, at the earliest, from the second half of 2017.

The start-up game is a tightrope walk. Any mistakes and the penalty is severe. In such a high pressure – high-tension, high-drama, high-stakes game, a delay in getting the promised funds is akin to fighting with eyes closed and hands tied behind your back and starving a rampaging army capable of stupendous blitzkrieg by cutting off its all-important supply lines.

Despite all the hardships, the business was doing good. We had three products now and the largest fashion brands were lining up to do trials with our AI-based cost and negotiation tool – the Intello3C. We were looking good to take on both the Wild Wild West and the Wild Wild East with our innovations.

However, I knew that we needed to raise more money or find a strong partner to expand the Intello3C business to the EU and US to conquer the fashion brands. The costs for sales and marketing in the EU and the US were astronomical compared to Asia, Africa and the Middle East. To deliver that, we needed more money and raising that would be the only option for delivering faster growth. The game was becoming increasingly tilted towards the ability to raise more money to deliver growth from the brand side in the West.

As we all sat around the bonfire on the beach and sang songs and told stories, I could not help but notice that our core team was intact, and the folks were happy. They believed that their work meant something.

Sitting and sipping my cold beer on the lovely North Goa beach, I had no inkling how our story was going to take another breathtaking turn, and it would be a 15-minute Bangkok gambit that would forever change the course of ThreadSol.

Name a place that's gaudy and sleazy
Bangkok – that's super easy!

19

The 15-Minute Bangkok Gambit

Bangkok, January 2017

Like most of the mega-sized Asian port cities – Manila, Jakarta, Hong Kong, Shanghai and Singapore – Bangkok has deeply religious and traditional social roots. Altruistic Buddhism mixed with the benevolence of Hinduism, the flash of Islam and the depth of Taoism is everywhere – in its arts, culture, architecture and music. And just like all the Asian port cities, there is the omnipresent traffic, overcrowding, bustling markets and the unmistakable sleaze. Yes, Bangkok is the sleaziest Asian port megacity and probably one of the sleaziest in the world.

In my dozen-plus business trips to the city, I have always stayed in the central Sukhumvit–Asoke area. Filled with towering business complexes and glittering malls, it feels like the modern corporate city centre. But, come nightfall, the same area dazzles with millions of neon lights and the go-go bars spring to life. The narrow roads fill up with curious tourists, boisterous regulars and a swathe of young, scantily clad women in gaudy makeup, trying to lure clients to their bars.

You cannot walk 10 steps without being accosted by someone suggesting you get a massage or a peek at their go-go bar. The first trip to Bangkok is most likely to make your head spin! The Soi Cowboy and Nana Plaza have the raunchiest shows in the town. And when you come out of the razzle-dazzle of this raunchy nightlife, you will notice that right in the middle of all of this is a small Buddhist pagoda lit with incense sticks and adorned with flowers.

Bangkok also has fantastic food. There are some seriously good rock and metal live band bars too. It is a very cosmopolitan city.

In January 2017, Mausmi and I landed in Bangkok. As we walked into the opulent Sheraton Grande, we were told that the managing director of Coats Global Services would only give us 15 minutes instead of the planned 90 minutes!

This was a serious blow. We had crafted a presentation that would showcase our products, people and processes in about 60 minutes and would leave 30 mins for discussions, etc. We hoped with this we could capture their imagination. What can you do in 15 minutes? It looked like our travel, preparations, etc. were going to be a big waste of time, money and effort.

Then Mausmi had a brainwave. She came up with the idea that probably changed the course of our business forever. It was a high-risk strategy but we decided to go for it.

There were 10 Brits sitting around the table in the boardroom where we had to make our presentation. Dave was there. Yael, the managing director was there as well. She was in her early forties, with lustrous blond hair and a piercing glance. An ex-Israel army lawyer by profession, she was hard as nails. Still, she seemed welcoming. We exchanged cards and shook hands with all the participants. Yael apologized for giving us only 15 minutes.

'Let's see what you guys have to show us. Do you have a presentation?' Yael asked.

'No, we do not,' Mausmi replied. 'Let's do a quick white board session.'

I went to the whiteboard and picked up a marker and delivered the content that Mausmi had come up with.

'Think of how a typical apparel brand works. Say, Nike has to manufacture 100 tees. First, they need to calculate how much fabric they need to buy to produce the 100 tees. Second, they need to plan how much time it would take them to make them. Third, they need to plan their factory's production lines and deliver the garments.'

I drew a simple flow chart with these three steps and continued.

'You guys are Coats – a $1.5 billion thread manufacturer. You have a software products division named Coats Global Services. You have acquired GSD and Fast React.

In the three steps of the flowchart I just drew, GSD solves the problem in step 2. GSD tells you how much time it will take to make the tees. Fast React solves the problem in step 3. It plans your production lines. But what about the first step? You have no solutions for this problem as of now,' I said and looked at the audience.

'We are the answer to the first step,' Mausmi said.

'Our solutions use artificial intelligence to predict how much fabric to buy and how to plan the fabric-cutting process. With us, you complete the holy trinity of solutions that all brands and manufacturers in the world are looking for. This is what we can do together. Thank you.'

We closed in five minutes!

The next 10 minutes went by in a flash. There were some questions about how many customers we had and how good our solution was and so on. We polished them off nicely. However, Yael, the MD, did not ask a single question. She sat there listening to all and maintained a studied silence.

She got up from her chair thanked us and off we went. We were standing in the lobby again – 15 minutes of whirlwind behind us!

It was a long silent walk back to our hotel. We had answered all the questions and presented our story quite well. But did we get too cocky in proposing that Coats must partner with us for their own good? Why was Yael so silent in the 15 minutes? Was she uninterested? Did she think we were too pushy?

We came back to our hotel and spent the late afternoon watching *The Big Bang Theory* to relax and wash off the 15-minute meeting. The funny antics of Sheldon Cooper and gang kept us in light spirits. We had planned to visit the Bangkok floating market in the evening. So, we went to have some tea around 4 p.m. A hot cup of Darjeeling tea always lifts my mood and as I sipped the warm golden liquid, it made me feel positive. And then my phone rang . . .

'Hey Manasij, this is Dave.' Dave was warm and loud and boisterous as usual.

'Hey Dave, how is it going?'

'Yes, all good. Hey look, Yael wants you guys to come over for the dinner. Are you guys free this evening for a dinner with us?'

We had our answer. We must have done well to turn a 15-minute meeting into a dinner. It meant that we would have to give the floating markets a miss, but neither of us was complaining.

We went back to Sheraton Grande for the dinner. It was a three-hour-long affair. The dinner conversation was mostly about how to build digitization and high-quality software solutions for the fashion industry. Yael sat with Mausmi and me and she was super chatty. She asked us lots of probing questions about our journey, our solution, our people and our future.

Nibbling on the scrumptious Thai food, the conversation took to lighter topics. We recounted some of our fun stories of building the business. At the end of the dinner as the last glasses of wine and brandy were doing the rounds, Yael leaned over and almost whispered into my ears, 'Do you guys come to London any time for business?'

'Yes, I am due to be in London in two weeks,' I replied. I had a London trip planned to meet the heads of Crystal Martin and Dewhirst, two billion-dollar-sized manufacturers, who were both about to sign a $200,000 deal with us.

'Good, then email me and we will sync up a time to meet.'

~

The thing that impresses me most about London is how the old and the new sort of mingle to become a modern, cosmopolitan metropolis. On one bank of the river Thames, you can see the 300-year-old theatre where Shakespeare used to host his plays and on the opposite side, you see fancy new condominiums. The new business districts glitter with glass and steel skyscrapers and 50 steps away, you can walk into a tavern that is 150 years old and still preserves its Victorian interiors.

Yael asked me to meet her in the 150-year-old Hospital Tavern, a stone's throw away from the Tower of London, where treasures from British colonies, including the famous Koh-i-Noor diamond, are on display. I was going into the meeting hoping that she would agree to take ThreadSol as a partner of Coats Global Services. Having a billion-dollar giant as a partner would be terrific – or so I thought.

The lunch was a lavish affair. Yael had great taste in food and drinks and she took charge of the ordering. Food was not big on my agenda as much as it was to get Yael to agree to partner with us. It is strange to be in setups like these. You are so focused on getting the outcome that everything else becomes secondary. With every sentence exchanged, I was intent on evaluating if the conversation was indeed going towards the goal.

Yael, however, had a knack for making people feel comfortable. She was clearly highly ambitious. She liked our strong focus on technology-driven problem-solving. She had this almost childlike excitement while discussing the possibilities of what tech could do to the business. As we ate our roast chickens, she dropped the bomb.

'You see, the presentation you guys did in Bangkok got me thinking that there are three pieces of the puzzle and we have covered two out of three. So, why not complete the picture and add the last piece to make a complete well-rounded three-pronged offering for the apparel brands and manufacturers?'

She then drew closer and almost whispered, 'How would you like to get acquired by Coats Global Services?'

I almost fell from my chair.

'I am sorry, could you repeat what you just said?' Frankly, I was not prepared for this question at all. Acquisition had never crossed my mind.

Yael laughed and repeated her statement.

'So Mausmi's gambit in Bangkok did make an impact!' I thought.

'Yes, surely the three joined pieces will make the whole thing so much better,' I said.

'Good. Then, let's call off this meeting. Let's not discuss work any more. I will be in touch for us to find a way to work ahead and look at the possibilities of acquiring you guys. I am not promising you anything, but this looks like the logical next step.'

We spent another 30 minutes at the table exchanging laughs and stories.

After the meeting, I took a long one-hour walk from the Hospital Tavern to my hotel on Strand Road through the north bank Thames riverside walkway. I could have easily taken the underground metro rail (or the tube as the Londoners affectionately call it), but I needed a walk and some fresh air to process the discussion.

I walked through open-air performances by street artists, tourists, food stalls and playing children. The ice-cold January wind hit my face and it felt refreshing. A rogue frisbee came flying towards me and I snapped it and returned it to a bunch of giggling mischievous young boys.

That late afternoon, I Skyped Mausmi, Abhishek and Bratish. I told them what Yael had said. My co-founding friends didn't do any better than what I had done in the Hospital Tavern. None of us had thought this engagement with Coats would open a possible channel for acquisition.

Our business was growing rapidly, and we were doing quite good. We had just raised the $3 million investment and we had done a topline of $1.8 million in 2016 and it looked good for us to build the business from here and scale it well. It was flattering to know that someone wanted us – or at the very least – deemed it worthy to discuss the prospect of acquiring us. This was a serious validation of the value of our work.

We decided to continue the engagement with Coats and see where it led. We agreed that it might not be a terrible idea to get acquired and we must keep our options open. We informed our investors.

Over the next few months, Yael initiated a lot of contact with various Coats teams. There were many rounds of product demos and detailed discussions on our marketing, sales, customer success and technology processes and a lot of data and information about our business and its financial metrics were shared and discussed.

It was Holi.

Mausmi and I had gone to Abhishek's place. After a sumptuous lunch, as we sat in the drawing room chatting and relaxing, I saw an unread email icon on my mobile.

'Hi Manasij,

I would like to propose a two-day working session in Colombo three weeks from now. I will invite Hizmy, the CTO of Coats, Dave, the head of GSD and Andrew, the head of Fast React. I would like all your founding team to be present.

Yael'

The game was on. And it was in Colombo, our lucky charm, the place where ThreadSol had kick-started its fortunes.

Looked like we were going to script a dream run.

20

Looks Like We Are Going to Script a Dream Run . . .

In a triangular tournament in 1998, Sachin Tendulkar was humiliatingly castled by a lethal bouncer from the Zimbabwean fast bowler Henry Olonga in Sharjah. A few days later, Sachin smashed the same bowler all around the ground in one of the finest displays of attacking batsmanship.

In 2001, at the EuroSpeedway Lausitz, Alex Zanardi, a fabulous moto racer who was leading the race with 13 laps to go, met with a horrific accident and lost both his legs. After extensive rehabilitation, Alex came back to the same track two years later and completed the remaining 13 laps in a specially modified car.

As an avid sports fan, I can tell you many such callback stories of getting defeated and then coming back to the same place against the same opposition and winning big. While we see plenty of callback moments in movies and novels, real-life callback moments are rare.

Three years ago, I found myself sitting in Colombo's Cinnamon Grand Hotel's ballroom during a symposium organized by Sri Lanka Design Festival.

The keynote speaker was Paul Foreman, the then CEO of Coats, who was a witty and charismatic speaker. After the session was over, he was mobbed by a big crowd, all wanting a piece of him. I was also in the crowd. I wanted to connect with Paul and ensure Coats kept us on their radar.

There is a secret about getting ahead in a crowd. The best way to understand this comes from the Chaos Theory. In a many-to-one interaction, where many want to get a piece of one, there will always be pandemonium. Chaos Theory suggests that even in the most disorderly system, a rare local minima will present itself every once in a while. So, when 30 people are screaming to get someone's attention, there will be a moment, however small, where the noise will subside and there will be a moment of rare silence. This is the moment that one needs to grab.

I had done something similar a few years back in Delhi's Siri Fort Auditorium during a film festival. I could not get tickets for Konkona Sen Sharma's acclaimed film *Dosar*. After trying all avenues, with no luck, I decided to accost Konkona when she was slated to come for the premiere. I went in with the crowd that had encircled Konkona and patiently waited for the local minima to present itself. It did and I went in.

I extended my palm for a handshake and looked directly into her eyes and said, 'Hey Konkona, I get 12 casual leaves a year and I took one to see this movie. However, I have no tickets. Can you please help?'

She was surprised. But she was gracious. She shook my hand and pointed to a group of folks, her entourage, and said, 'You are welcome to hang with them. They are my friends and are here to watch the show. Hopefully, you can get in with them?'

I did just that. I hung around with her fashionable entourage as a 'friend of Konkona' and went into the hall to get the box seats with free beverages and snacks and enjoyed the movie.

As I jostled with 20 others in Colombo's Cinnamon Grand Hotel's ballroom to get Paul's attention, I waited for the local minima to present itself. And as expected, it did. I went in and extended my palm and said, 'Hey Paul, I am a nobody, and I am building an AI-driven start-up that works for the largest fashion brands and manufacturers and saves them millions of dollars. I would love to work with Coats.'

Paul was gracious and welcoming and introduced me to his team. But the result was not as stellar as getting a box seat. So, when in the summer of 2017, I walked into the same resplendent ballroom again, this time for a two-day meeting with Coats, and my callback moment was complete.

After two days of hectic meetings, it was clear that Coats was serious about doing the acquisition. On the last day of our meetings, we sat around the lovely outdoor restaurant of the Cinnamon Grand and feasted on the excellent Sri Lankan crabs and other seafood.

The biggest crabs were listed on the menu as Crabzilla. The claws were as big as a baby's arm! We dug into the seafood and conversed. In the middle of dinner, Yael invited us to the UK for a serious discussion on the acquisition terms and price, etc.

'Look guys, I will be on maternity leave from next week for the next six months. In my absence, Hizmy, the CTO of Coats, will be the deal champion for this acquisition. I am sure we can quickly complete the deal and that's why you guys should come to the UK in the next month.'

It was bit of a shock that Yael would be off work, but then everything looked positive, and it was a great next step to be invited to the UK for a final discussion on the deal.

Looked like we were going to script a dream run.

Agra. Again!

From the rooftop of our hotel, we had an unhindered view of the majestic Taj Mahal. It was a full moon night and we could see the white marble bathed in brilliant silver moonlight. On these nights, the Taj Mahal glows in a ghostly blueish tinge – a truly mesmerizing sight. The monument allows only 200 visitors in these three nights to see it up close. Since we had made the plans at the very last minute, we missed those highly coveted tickets. To compensate, Abhishek had booked the four of us in the luxurious Oberoi Amarvilas Hotel, which had the best views of the Taj. On this full moon night, it looked like a million bucks.

We had come to Agra for one day to talk about what we wanted to do. In the next few weeks, we were slated to fly to the UK to discuss the prospective acquisition with Coats. All four of us were caught up in our day-to-day work of running the business and we thought coming to Agra for a day would be a good way to get uninterrupted time for us to have a deeper conversation.

It felt surreal that the four of us were having this conversation in this setup. I think all my co-founders were overwhelmed by the occasion too. Other than the Coats story of acquisition, one of the most prolific VC funds of India, SAIF Partners (now Elevation Capital), who had invested into well-known Indian start-ups like BookMyShow, MakeMyTrip, Ixigo, Paytm, Swiggy, Urban Company, Unacademy, etc. wanted to invest in us as well. The discussions were in advanced rounds of raising $10 million from them. We were in a good position of having two options.

On one hand, raising $10 million would be fantastic for the business and we could deploy the funds to accelerate our business and look to create an outpost in the US or the UK to work with the apparel brands. On the other hand, there was Coats, a billion-dollar giant with deep-deep-deep pockets and deep-deep-deep connections in the fashion industry, that could take our story to much bigger heights much faster than just through the capital-driven acceleration we would get from investor money.

On one hand, if we went with Coats, it would mean we relinquish control over the business that we had built with our blood, sweat and tears and Coats would drive the story from thereon while we could possibly play valuable roles in shaping the future. On the other hand, we could ingest the VC money and keep our business under our watch and look for growth avenues.

If we raised another round of investment, the company valuation would rise from the current $10 million. The subsequent sale further down the line would mean the next buyer would have to pay almost $50–$100 million for our business.

We knew full well that there were no parallels of an apparel tech start-up having made an exit through M&A worldwide. Therefore, delaying the exit, which invariably means a much bigger exit value down the road, makes the case that much more unlikely as we would have to believe that we would be able to go against the market dynamics and get an outcome that has never happened worldwide. However, if we sold now, surely we would have to settle with a lower acquisition value.

Yes, we were growing strongly and the business looked very healthy. We could remain bullish that this dizzying growth, something the apparel tech sector has never seen before, would continue and we would be able to raise more capital and exit really big. However, just because this was such a nascent sector, there were no sureties that this would happen.

There were no easy answers. Whatever we chose seemed not optimum. Running a start-up is a delicate balancing act. There are seductive calls of glory and big bucks and associated stardom but there is always this chance of a grim fall from grace and ending up with an unnamed grave on the battlefield.

There are stories where the founders didn't sell despite a big offer on the table and made the companies even bigger and acquired legendary celebrity status. But for every such story, there are thousands of unknown stories where some defiant founder didn't take the offer only to see the business they built vanish into thin air and become drunk nostalgia in some dimly lit pub.

The desperation and guilt of thousands of founders are always buried in the basements of the towering multi-billion-dollar success of a few poster boys.

You know all of this as a founder. And you think, when such an opportune moment arrives, you will be the one to take the right step. You believe that you will be the one to beat the odds – you will come up trumps. But, the thing is, when you are in that situation, you just don't know. Period. You can never be sure. So, should you collect your winnings, cash out and go home a winner to get a chicken dinner or should you bet it all again and push the slot lever one more time? I guess, this classic conundrum will be one of those unsolved issues.

Abhishek, Bratish, Mausmi and I discussed these threadbare. It was a funny discussion. We vacillated from one side to the other and if there was a fly on the wall, it would have thought we were a naïve, undecided bunch who had no business running a business. We quickly realized that both the options looked equally good and equally bad and we had no data or evidence at hand to make a judgment based on facts.

It was all down to the gut. So, we focused inwards. What did we want from this journey in the first place? Did we want money? Fame? Glamour? No. We wanted to build something that was an expression of our collective creativity and we hoped it would be our small pebble-sized contribution to the enduring edifice of relentless human progress.

'So, it is decided, we will go ahead with Coats and try to get this acquisition to a logical point.' Bratish summed up our whole evening-long conversation. He was the most gutted of all. He is a straight arrow and wants to make all decisions based on pure logic, and it was quite agonizing for him that there was almost no data to base his opinion on.

Abhishek was much more relaxed. He has this boundless urn of positivity to dip into.

'Look at the bright side. Not many can boast of building a category creator business and making an exit to a multi-billion-dollar-sized organization. We will be one.'

Mausmi was glum.

'I never thought we would sell. I thought we could build and build and build.'

I could sympathize with her. ThreadSol was her idea.

I was a mix of emotions. My mind had drifted to another problem at hand. Convincing the investors to go ahead with the sale would be hard, given that we were growing strongly. I could almost hear Karthik say in his usual baritone, 'Yeah, you can sell, but it won't be worth a book.' And there was the question of agreeing on the valuation, the terms of the deal, and all the other stuff.

I was firmly of the opinion from day one that we build the business with an eye for an acquisition down the line. Acquisitions and IPOs are the only two benchmarks of a successful journey. You return money manifold to the investors. You build a business from scratch and take it to a logical conclusion. In our case, there was no history of any acquisitions of any apparel tech start-ups anywhere in the world. We would be the first. That's a great vindication of our product, our team and our tenacity. I favoured the acquisition route.

As we all stood at the edge of the roof and marvelled at the Taj Mahal's beauty, Abhishek said, 'Looks like we are going to script a dream run . . .'

Today when we recall this, we all share a hearty laugh.

It was all too good to be true . . .

21

It Was All Too Good to Be True . . .

Windsor, UK. August 2017.

A shining Mercedes had picked us up from Heathrow Airport and 45 minutes later, we were checking into a 500-year-old inn, bang opposite Windsor Castle, that had been converted into a fabulous hotel. Coats had flown us business class from Delhi and despite a nine-hour haul, the lovely flatbed and the pampering service meant we were feeling energized and fresh.

We had some good laughs at the New Delhi airport though. As the four of us approached the business class boarding queue, an officer stopped me and asked me to move to the economy queue. I was dressed in my usual shorts and tee and he rightly profiled my clothing as unbecoming to be at the front of the plane.

I didn't feel bad at all. He was right after all. I have always been an economy class traveler to save as much as we could and barring a few fortunate upgrades, my experience with business class was wafer-thin.

The Windsor hotel was super cute. The décor was unmistakably Victorian, and the construction was mostly all wood. The rooms were small but cozy and the meeting room, which was booked for the next three days, was tiny. The agenda was clear. Day one

The Queen blesses – we struck a deal
It fizzles out – how does it feel?

was all about our products, people and processes. Day two was about finding the common ground on valuation and drafting the joint business plan. Day three would be the day when the Coats CXOs would meet us to bless the deal if everything prior to that checked out.

The Coats team was being led by Hizmy, the CTO of Coats, standing in absence of Yael. The contingent had their head of acquisitions Judith, head of accounts Rob, Yael's second-in-command Glenn and a few guest appearances for tech, finance, marketing, etc. Hizmy, Judith, Rob and Glenn were staying in the same hotel for the next three days. This meant that every day began with them at the breakfast table and after nine–ten hours of marathon meetings, we ended with them at the dinner table. There was too much overlap. The only time the four of us would get to confer among ourselves would be once the day got over – pretty much near midnight.

The beginning was less than auspicious. As Yael was absent, we had to almost start from scratch with this team. The room was a cornucopia of strange accents. Hizmy was a Sri Lankan expat, now a UK citizen, in his early fifties, who spoke in a difficult Sri Lankan accent. Glenn's accent was clearly screaming of the midlands. He was a giant, almost six foot four. But, Rob was still taller, probably six foot eight and spoke with such a thick southern British accent that I was tempted to ask for a translator who could translate his English to English.

Judith was probably from France or Belgium and had a French English accent. And we four had our Indian English. It felt like being at a UN convention. Only at the UN conventions, everyone knows that no clear objective is achievable.

Day one was a success. The team understood what we were doing and was very appreciative. The dinner conversation was also a lot of fun. We went to a nearby restaurant by the river that had excellent steaks and wine. We felt that things were going fine.

Day two was all about finding the right acquisition price and the joint business plan with Coats. The day began on an inexplicably shrill note. We felt like a pressure cooker put on a boil on a slow burner. I could see Abhishek, Bratish and Mausmi getting more and more bewildered as they were unable to understand why the meeting was slowly but surely turning hostile. Having been through many negotiations with many business owners, I knew this was just a tactic to get the price they wanted. So, despite being pushed to the edge, we stayed calm and weathered the storm.

The lunch was a silent affair. As we came out for some fresh air, we saw the colourful royal guards march to the palace through the streets right in front of our hotel. The Castle had the Union Jack flying high, a sign that today the Queen was in residence in the palace. It was a lovely sunny afternoon. It would have been a great day to sit on a lush meadow with a picnic lunch and a board of Scrabble.

Instead, we went back to the small room. The Coats team was already waiting for us and the silence in the room was deafening. Rob presented their tentative valuation proposal. Finally, the cat was out of the box. We rejected it outright.

An hour passed with nothing meaningful being agreed on. I moved for a 15-minute adjournment. They accepted. The four of us came out to the streets. The previous night after dinner, we had discussed the possibility of being offered a low-balled valuation. We had discussed and decided on the no-go-mark and now the team put me in charge of bringing this home.

Back in the room, it seemed the Coats team had also debriefed and regrouped. In the next four hours or so, the day was to come to an end. So, the next four hours were crucial. These would define the way ahead. Surely, the big bosses wanted an update on the progress and surely, they wanted a deal. We knew it. They knew it. We knew that they knew, and they knew that we knew that they knew. Yep, take a moment to wrap your head around that!

As I was entering the meeting room, I saw my WhatsApp – SAIF partners had moved the ball ahead and we had an invitation from the $40 billion apparel trading company Li & Fung to trial our solution Intello3C parallelly in Hong Kong, Shanghai and Shenzhen. These were great developments. We should play on the front foot.

The next three hours were a pure logjam. It was like fencing where you advance with the sword towards your opponent, but you just don't get to score, and then your opponent does the same.

Let me switch to Mausmi's narration to explain this part better.

Rob presented another impossible number. I saw Manasij shoot him down while he did some board work with the group on how we could get a better outcome by just raising another round of VC money. In our break time, Manasij had mentioned that this would go down the wire and the number would be finally agreed upon, if at all, at the dying minutes of today's meeting schedule.

As Rob, Judith, Glenn and Manasij were wrestling with the Excel numbers, Hizmy was messaging on his phone, his hands below the table so he couldn't be seen. As the logjam continued, I counted how many times he did this – one, two, three times. Surely, he was in some discussion with the high-ups. He was not looking happy.

Every time he did that, I would also put my hand below the table to show Manasij the count with my fingers. Three and a half hours went by. The meeting was to end in the next 30 minutes. There were some agreements about the deal process. It was agreed that this would be an all-cash deal and no share component would be attached. Typically, in a sale, the purchaser pays part cash and part through their shares. It was agreed that all our employees would continue to be under Coats' employment. Only one thing was still stuck – the total deal value. 30 minutes before the close of the meeting, I saw Hizmy duck his hand under the table for another round of message exchange. I counted on my finger too. Five!

And then Hizmy sat up straight on his chair.

'Manasij, we need to close this today or we shall call it off.'

'Don't worry if he offers a threat. A threat means he has to close this,' Manasij had told us during the break. 'If he doesn't want the deal, he would let it hang rather than try to close. We have to wait until that time. Until we see the abyss. Anything before that, you undersell.'

In the next 15 minutes, what ensued, can only be best called a market. They both started at two ends of the stick and then they converged on a number.

Manasij: '45'

Hizmy: '22'

Manasij: '40'

Hizmy: '24'

Manasij: '35'

Hizmy: '25'

Manasij: '30'

Hizmy: '27'

Manasij: '30' (he stressed it strongly)

Hizmy: '30'

We had a deal!

$30 million!

₹220 crore!

Wow!

Last night, we had agreed that $25 million all-cash would be a decent outcome. Our current valuation was around $10 million or so. This was above that. I knew Manasij was happy with the *outcome. However, Hizmy was not. He probably had a lower number in his head. His face was red and coated with sweat.*

When Manasij and Hizmy shook hands, the tension showed.

Hizmy: 'Well you negotiated hard.'

Manasij: 'That's okay, Hizmy, it is a part of the game.'

Hizmy: 'This was no game.'

Manasij: (smiles)

The smiles were back at dinner. I was exhausted. The nine hours of negotiations had drained me. Abhishek, Bratish and Mausmi were also emotionally drained. But there were smiles on their faces. I do not recall much of the discussion except that Yael had come to see us. It was a Russian-run pub in Central London where we had all gone to wash off the day. She was delighted and hugged us as she came into the pub. I remember doing a Russian accent imitation that drew laughter from Glen, Hizmy and Yael. The rack of lamb tasted great.

The next day was more or less a procession of formality. The camaraderie and appreciations were back in the game. Adrian Elliott, Yael's boss and the CEO's right-hand man, paid a visit to the meeting. He was in his mid-fifties and lean and tall – almost six foot. He had sparkling eyes and used humour as a weapon. We discussed the details of the deal, the next steps and so on. He was there to prepare the deck for Coats' CEO's visit to the meeting. That was contingent on all agreements being in place. Something really funny happened when Rajiv Sharma, the CEO of Coats, came to the meeting.

'Rajiv is coming . . . Rajiv is coming . . .'

A nervous excitement swept through the room. Everyone at once assumed an upright posture and looked serious and in walked Rajiv, dressed immaculately in a super formal grey suit. He was in his mid-fifties, five foot ten, heavily built with a bald head, wearing rimless glasses. He sat down and said, 'Okay, catch me up.' I could almost hear the collective sigh of relief from his colleagues. The room was breathing again. The room began to hum again. We found this quite funny. How many times have I walked into a room full of my colleagues and they have got this uptight? It was funny to witness this.

The last dinner was a lavish affair. Rajiv sat opposite me. He asked me questions after questions.

'Do you feel more excited to start a project or when you end one?'

'What excites you more, technological brilliance or hard-nosed execution?'

'What animal would you describe ThreadSol as?'

From his viewpoint, these must have been probing questions. I thought they were funny. We had built the business from scratch, risked dying twice, worked super hard to build, scale, establish ourselves. How did it matter what animal I think we were? But the thing is, the deal was still not over. So, I gave him the answers that he wanted to hear than what I thought would be the real ones.

'Do you feel more excited to start a project or when you end one?'

Of course, I felt more excited to begin. When you end one, you feel relief.

But I said, 'I feel more excited to see a good journey to its logical well-earned conclusion.' It was also a truthful answer but surely not my first choice answer to the question.

'What excites you more, technological brilliance or hard-nosed execution?'

I would have said I am a techie at heart. The possibilities of tech excite me each day.

But I said, 'I think without execution, everything fizzles out. I rate that highly on my scales.'

'What animal you would describe ThreadSol as?'

I had never thought what animal we were. And why would I? What good would that bring anyway?

But I said, 'I think ThreadSol is an ant colony. We co-operate and work in unison to bring our objectives home.'

I felt like I was in a beauty pageant, being forced to answer endless meaningless questions. But then, when you are selling your start-up, maybe you are in a beauty pageant after all.

The next day we went back to Delhi. I wore my jeans on the way back so that the airport officers would not harass me to join the economy class queue again!

The next four months were a serious drag. Every day there were long tiring calls with various teams from Coats, lawyers, finance people, marketing people, HR folks, global salespeople, technical team members, accounting team, health and safety team, this team, that team, this honcho, that honcho.

A swarm of DD officers descended on us. DD is the process that precedes every major investment and acquisition. Through the DD processes, the investor or the acquirer finds out anything and everything about the business they are going to acquire/invest in.

These de-risk their position and make them aware if anything is a cause for concern, or if the business is run legally with proper controls and compliance and there are no red flags in any of its functioning. Depending on the complexity of the business and the zeal of the DD surveyors, this can last a few weeks to many months.

The DD reports present the worst of you. The DD surveyors have no skin in the game. They are mostly big consultancy firms like KPMG, PWC, E&Y and Deloitte, and they bill on time spent. So, they will happily extend a DD process until the last star dies in the universe. It is therefore the DD commissioning party's prerogative, in this case, Coats' prerogative, to control and limit this.

In one case the DD report flagged that we had no ambulance number given in any of the common areas and in case of a serious workplace injury, this could mean death and disability for the injured. Now, this became quite an issue as Coats is serious about health and safety. It makes sense for them to be so as they manufacture thread and there are moving machines and there is a possibility of workplace injury. In our case, we were a software company. The only injury you could get here was being hit by a ping-pong ball in the basement play area. I let you be the judge if keeping an ambulance number handy for that would be necessary or prudent.

In any case, it was up to Coats to control these and to take a pragmatic approach to tide over these small bumps. However, there was a wrinkle. With Yael on maternity leave, the decision-making at Coats was slow and painful. There was no one-window clearance. So, the DD was getting dragged. Often, we would get the impression that an issue is closed, and we could move on, only to see its resurgence four weeks down the line through some other channels. This was becoming the order of the engagement.

There were other associated costs too. With all four founders and the head of all departments getting caught up in this DD storm, the business was starting to suffer. Often, in start-ups, the gamekeepers and housekeepers are the same folks. After two months of DD, our quarter results were starting to show signs of stress. This made the Coats team nervous and again without Yael, who was the deal champion, these small deviations were causing us to get into meetings that were not warranted.

By late November 2017, almost four months into the DD, I

started to get a feeling that we were walking in circles and even backwards. The acquisition was losing momentum and so were we. We posted a bad quarter. It was 15 per cent below expectation.

The final nail in the coffin came on the first of December 2017. I was in Hong Kong to close the pilot of Intello3C with Li & Fung and met their MD and CEO patriarch Victor Fung. We were to begin the trials with six of their brand divisions in Hong Kong, Shanghai and Shenzhen. We had posted fantastic early results and Li & Fung was looking at saving in tunes of $100 million a year with our solution.

The pilots were the next logical step. If they succeeded, we could look for a deal potentially in millions of dollars a year. I was spending my full working days in the Hong Kong Li & Fung office in various meetings. And I would start getting into the DD calls from 6 in the evening when London woke up as it was eight hours behind Hong Kong. The calls would extend up to 4 in the morning!

In one fateful call, we had our lawyers from India and Singapore present; Coats had their lawyers from India, Singapore, Indonesia and Vietnam (two countries where we had our subsidiaries present). From our side, all four founders, the head of operations of all countries, and our finance head were also present. Our investors Blume and Catamaran also had their lawyers.

From Coats' side, their DD team and the UK legal team were also present along with Hizmy and Judith. All together around 40 people! What ensued was an unbelievable four-hour legal blitz where the only thing of substance that the legal DD team had to put was their apprehension of some future tax law changes (that hasn't happened even today and is not likely to happen in the near future). Hizmy and Judith were no legal experts, and they chose to play it safe, as every high-ranking executive would, and leave it to the squabbling lawyers to make sense.

'This is going nowhere.' I saw Bratish's message on our WhatsApp group.

'I agree,' Abhishek replied.

'What can we do?' Mausmi asked.

'I think we need to call quits,' I wrote.

I had a quick call with Hizmy after this. He was at sea. He had no understanding of the issue and though he agreed that whatever the logjam was, it had to do with some future possible event; he had no incentives to go against the ultra-conservative 'legal opinion'.

'Manasij, from 20 December, every one of us will be going on year-end leave. If we cannot close by then, this will reopen when we come back in mid-January. Decide what you want to do.' He was clearly not willing to take a stand and see things home.

So, I convened the founding group one more time over a Skype call at 4 a.m. in Hong Kong, 1.30 a.m. in India!

'Guys, here is the situation. I think Yael's absence has hurt the whole thing. No head of state can bring this home in Coats now. We can continue to struggle with them as we have for the last almost four–five months, until Yael comes back to work in April 2018, or we call it quits and focus on our business. As of now, our valuable time and resources are neck deep trying to win a losing battle here while the business has started to lose. We have this huge Li & Fung pilot coming up. And it seems in January/February, SAIF Partners could also close on the investment discussions.'

I looked at the tired expressions of my friends and felt bad for them. They had done everything from their side to pull this together.

'So, I am suggesting we pull the plug. Call it quits. Go home,' I said.

A long silence ensued. Everyone was pensive. It was a lot of effort wasted, a lot of time wasted, a lot of opportunities wasted and a lot of money wasted. For a small start-up, this was a terrible cost to pay. And it is not just the dollar cost – the time and opportunity costs were the bigger drains. If we stayed on, the costs would mount and might just cripple us. Pulling out seemed like the logical choice.

Thirty minutes later, I sent a short mail asking Coats to pause the DD – thanking them for their love and support and suggesting they look at us down the line.

It was almost 5 a.m., I was awake the whole night. I came out of the hotel and stood on the pavement. I have always stayed at the same hotel – Hotel Shamrock (unlike its name, it doesn't rock and as the name suggests, it is quite a sham) on Nathan Road near the glitzy shopping district of Tsim-Tsa-Tsui. The city was still in its night garb. Roads were empty. One or two vehicles would occasionally pass. The street-cleaning trucks were making their nocturnal sweeps on the roads and the alleys. The neon lights of the street flickered all around me. As I stood there and lit a cigarette, I felt a strange cocktail of emotions.

'Do you feel more excited to start a project or when you end one?'

I recalled the question from Rajiv, the Coats CEO a few months back and chuckled.

I don't know man; I feel pretty bad to leave things half done. How about you? I shook my head.

It was a painful time. I was sad that the acquisition didn't go through. I was sad that it took so much of our attention and left us poorer. I was sad that we suffered a bad quarterly result because of this colossal distraction.

How will I explain this dip to a prospective investor? I wondered.

On the other hand, I was relieved that we would not have to endure more meaningless meetings and calls with make-believe issues. I was relieved that we could focus on our business again with all gusto. I was relieved that an investor and big prospective deals were waiting in the folds to partner with us.

'It was all too good to be true.'

Bratish's parting words in the Skype call echoed in my head as I went back to my room to get a few hours of shut-eye.

But sleep eluded me. What if I could run to the UK and meet up with all the folks and fix all these issues? Did I act in haste? Did I act too late? Did I do something wrong here? Have I let down my folks? I kept tossing and turning in my hotel bed. I was restless as hell.

And with that Coats was gone. We were back to the grind. The team took the news with surprising ease. I was elated to see the folks snap back to the game with full enthusiasm. This time at the year-end, ThreadSol went to a lovely Rajasthani haveli called the Chomu Palace. A few days with the team was just what we needed.

The year 2017 had one last sting in the tail though. One of our big group deals in an Indonesian group stalled. We were completely at sea. We had done six months of hard work to make that deal happen and at the last moment, it slipped away. It was a six-factory deal of $300,000. Ankit, our guy in Indonesia, discovered the reason. The factory group had employed an Indian development agency in Chennai to copy our solution in the six months of trials that we ran.

No, the copy could not get the required savings in dollar terms, but the tech head was boasting of it nonetheless. It was highly unethical. One problem with this apparel industry was its unethical malpractices and we had always remained a straight arrow. The right option was to file a legal case. But then Indian courts have millions of pending cases. Galileo was awarded the case that the Earth indeed went around the sun. It took 350 years for the Vatican to vindicate Galileo. Indian courts could take longer –

we just didn't have the time. So, I took a different approach. I met the founder of this Chennai company and offered to buy him out. He took it. We acquired his company for $30,000 and we were back in the hunt. I was now a true-blood entrepreneur. I knew which door to kick and which door to knock on. But this cost us precious revenue and time – the mortal enemy of an entrepreneur!

As 2018 rolled in, we were feeling positive again. We raked in $3 million in sales in 2017, and despite all the distractions of this long-drawn Coats DD, we reached the target that we had set ourselves at the start of the year. If the DD process had been any smoother, we could have done more. The acquisition would have been a terrific story too.

It's time to move on. It was never meant to be. It was too good to be true.

Who knew that the next six months would be dominated by one word?

No! Nope! Nein! Niyet! Naah!

Aliens, King Kong, Godzilla and all visited New York – now ThreadSol…

22

No! Nope! Nein! Nyet! Naah!

Hong Kong, February 2018

It was 3 in the morning. Yamini, Jasleen, Mausmi and I were all awake. Our tiny Hong Kong hotel room was a mess. Our laptops, notebooks, xerox copies of documents, printouts, hand-drawn charts, half-eaten pizza boxes, chips, consumed soft drinks – all were strewn around like dead bodies from a bloody warzone.

'Savings of 100 million dollars a year?' I was gasping for breath, 'Are we sure this is the number we are getting? It is huge.' I mused.

We had gone through collating the data from the three-month pilot exercise of Intello3C, our AI-driven costing system, for Li & Fung. Li & Fung is a $40 billion group that manages the supply chain of almost 500 apparel brands worldwide. We had done a three-month pilot with them in New Delhi, Dhaka, Hong Kong, Shanghai and Shenzhen. With an analysis of over 2,000 data points, Intello3C was projecting a $100 million a year saving for Li & Fung. It was huge. The quantum shocked and scared me.

Yamini and Jasleen – two of the finest of ThreadSol's indomitable women – were leading these pilots under Mausmi's aegis. Both had incredible energy and towering presence in a client space, and they had done a fantastic job running a thoroughly professional pilot with this humungous-sized corporate beast.

In fact, Yamini was taken ill with food poisoning just a night before and she had spent the whole night in the Emergency Room of Prince Edwards Hospital in Hong Kong. She was released at 6 in the morning and rather than staying in bed, she turned up for the 8 a.m. meeting with the Li & Fung vice president. When one of the folks asked how our evening was, she dismissed the whole night's ordeal with one word – 'uneventful' – and focused the conversation back to the agenda. Yes, Yamini was a total badass and she was scary when it came to work. We all loved her for that though!

We were doing similar pilots with large billion-dollar-sized apparel brands such as PVH, Adidas, Tchibo, Under Armour, Kiabi, Ralph Lauren, Nike and Helley Hansen. Intello3C was posting fantastic results in each of these places, but Li & Fung was the mother of all.

We all went out for a walk by the bayside at 4 a.m. after completing the work. We had a great chance of getting Li & Fung to adopt our solution on the back of these fantastic savings. I was tasked to bring the deal home.

Great! It was just one more meeting with the honchos and we were home!

It looked within our grasp – after all, who in their right mind would not take a deal that good?

New York, March 2018

I was sitting on the 41st floor of 12 East, 49th Street – five minutes from the fabled Times Square and right at the heart of the big apple's financial district. I was meeting the Zephyr Group, based in India, Sri Lanka and the US, as they were looking at investing in us. It was for $10 million ask. They had trekked to our customer sites and conducted interviews to understand why we were special. Finally, they had invited me to New York to seal the deal.

The meeting was with the partners of the IC. The IC is the final decision body for any investment. It consists of the partners and the senior members of the fund who vote on each prospective investment. The deal teams bring the investment thesis to the IC and if the IC likes it and it gets a majority vote, the deal is given a green signal.

The meeting went down as smoothly as an aged single malt. The partners were agreed on the opportunity. Broad terms were discussed and agreed upon. They wanted to check with our existing investors for one last step and then it would be a done deal. They were getting a good stake in ThreadSol. We were getting a $10 million Series B investment – all bright and sunny!

It looked within our grasp – after all, who in their right mind would not take a deal that good?

Gurgaon, April 2018

Abhishek, Bratish, Mausmi and I were sitting in the resplendent boardroom of SAIF Partners.

We had been invited to the IC finalizing the deal with the partners. Abhishek, Bratish, Mausmi and I endured a two-hour commute from Noida to reach their office.

Our deal champion told me, 'Don't worry, Manasij. We are in very good shape. Stay cool and this will be done. We have evaluated many companies but I can tell you that I have not seen many companies that have such strong customer love and give such strong value to the customers.'

Great! It was just one more meeting with the IC and we are home!

It looked within our grasp – after all, who in their right mind would not take a deal that good?

Walter Alvarez, a professor in the Earth and Planetary Science Department at the University of California, Berkeley, was exasperated. He was trying to solve the oldest murder mystery on the planet – what killed the big dinosaurs? Around the world, palaeontologists looking for fossils have found dinosaurs from 210 million years ago right until you hit 65 million years. After that, guess what? No dinos! It was as if they just vanished into thin air.

While visiting Gubbio in Italy, Alvarez noticed a thin but unmistakable grey sediment layer in the exposed rock faces. The layer created a boundary between the Cretaceous and Tertiary periods (known as the KT boundary) – it was the same boundary seen in every sedimentary rock formation. Below this boundary, you saw dinosaur fossils. Above this boundary – none!

Walter Alvarez postulated that the KT boundary represented a major asteroid that hit Earth and wiped out 75 per cent of the planet's life including the mighty dinosaurs. He showed evidence after evidence for this theory. The evidence of Iridium, an element we get mostly from asteroids, could be found in the KT boundary. There was also evidence of giant tsunamis dating 65 million years, about the time the asteroid hit Earth.

So what did he hear from the experts?

No! Nope! Nein! Nyet! Naah!

However, over time as more facts were uncovered, Alvarez's theory came to be accepted as the most likely reason for the dino's disappearance.

Running a start-up, however, is not fully science. The biggest problem is, in start-ups, no one has the time to show that they were right eventually. Time doesn't favour start-ups. If a customer moves on now, it is hard to get them later. If an investor escapes now, they are gone forever. So, unlike Walter Alvarez, who could painstakingly collect all the data and evidence and hope to be proven right in due course, we had no such opportunity. For us, it was now or never!

My meeting with Li & Fung in Hong Kong failed spectacularly. Why? Why would they not take our innovation that could save them $100 million a year? Two reasons – one, the $100 million saving number was too big and accepting such a big number made their existing process look highly suboptimal, even bordering stupid. And two, it begs the question why, despite tens of millions of dollars of IT and development budget, Li & Fung couldn't develop such a tool themselves? I saw the meeting torpedoed by the CIO.

'Manasij, for such large numbers, you need someone from the topmost echelons of Li & Fung to make this happen. This is too threatening for many. You should start this from the Western Hemisphere. That's where the real decision-making of brands would be,' one of the well-wishers, who was an insider at Li & Fung, told me.

We learnt that for such large deals, we needed internal political manoeuvring and corporate navigation. That was a revelation!

So, what did Li & Fung finally say?

No! Nope! Nein! Nyet! Naah!

And what did the Zephyr guys say? Well, that was one funny story. They called our existing investors. Blume said great things about us and confirmed they would participate in the next round of fundraising. However, Catamaran was not clear in giving a thumbs up. They did not commit to participating in the fundraising.

That spooked Zephyr and they backed out. Why did Catamaran do this? Catamaran had some regulatory issues stopping them from investing in an overseas business (remember we were now a Singapore-based business), and rather than being clear about this handicap, they decided to stay non-committal and that killed the deal. I do not blame anyone. Sometimes things just fall into a hole, and you have to accept it.

So, what did Zephry finally say?

No! Nope! Nein! Nyet! Naah!

And what did SAIF Partners say? Well, something funny happened there too. The deal team was so enthused by ThreadSol that they produced a long investment thesis document instead of the regular super-concise one. So, the busy IC members, who probably opened the investment thesis an hour before the meeting expecting a quick read, got a long read instead! And guess what happened because of that? It bombed our meeting! Again, they were great guys – thorough professionals and though the deal didn't happen, I am still good friends with the folks. We all know these yes-es and no-s are part of the game. No hard feelings.

So, what did SAIF Partners finally say?

No! Nope! Nein! Nyet! Naah!

In May 2018, we had our cultural night. Folks recited their poetry. A few stand-up performances tickled everyone. The band played five–six songs. The dance group made everyone tap their feet. It was a super fun night and to cap it, the night ended in a refreshing and violent thunderstorm.

As we all sat on the rain-drenched office stairs and sipped chilled beer, I heard my phone ring.

It was a WhatsApp from Yael.

'Hey Manasij, I am back to work after my maternity leave. We are thinking about restarting the acquisition discussions.' Yael was back with her go-getter style.

'Hey, Yael, great to hear from you. Weren't we on a break?' I replied. I knew Yael loved the sitcom, *Friends*.

'Haha, let's bring this home. It is a Ross-Rachel story . . .'

23

It Is a Ross-Rachel Story!

Ho Chi Minh City, Vietnam. June 2018.

What strikes any first-time visitor about this mega-metropolis is its incredible population of two-wheelers. There are bikes and scooters everywhere. On a four-lane street, three lanes will be occupied by bikes and scooters, leaving only one lane for cars. The second noticeable thing about this fantastic city is its terrific eating-out culture. Almost everywhere there are restaurants, street-side sit-out joints, pop-up food stalls and super-sized tin-shed eateries serving 300+ customers with delectable Vietnamese food. Come evenings, Vietnamese people throng these eateries that are surprisingly affordable. And the beer is surprisingly cheap too!

I had been to Vietnam a dozen times or so for ThreadSol business and we had a subsidiary of our Singapore company here. Saurav had relocated to Saigon (another name for Ho Chi Minh City) and had taken a lovely airy three-bedroom flat in District 5. I would always stay with him when I visited.

Vietnam impressed me immensely. The work culture was professional. It was young with huge female participation. The role of women in Vietnam was very strong. The decades-long war with the US had seen a huge loss of men and women had thus ascended to power positions.

Eventually, the women joined the fight too. North Vietnam, which used to be the guerrilla stronghold, had built a jungle trail route called the Ho Chi Minh Road that transected North Vietnam, Laos, Cambodia and entered South Vietnam (US stronghold). Over the years, more bombs were dropped by the US on this trail than the total bombs dropped in the entire World War II. The women used to drive trucks through this treacherous mountainous jungle dirt track.

They were supposed to drive without headlamps at night so that the US bombers could not target them. The women drove in a relay format. Each woman drove for 20 kilometres before passing on to the next woman and took a returning truck to her starting point. They had to memorize the route so that they could drive at night. The spirited fight ended in an embarrassing defeat for the US and since then Vietnam became united and is now one of the fastest-growing economies in Southeast Asia.

We had a thriving business in Vietnam. It was the third largest apparel manufacturing country in the world, after China and Bangladesh. And the growing business meant I would keep coming back. But this June, Mausmi and I were there for something else.

We were meeting the Coats' general executive team, or GET. The GET met every few months all around the world and took important strategic decisions. We had 30 minutes with them to rekindle the acquisition discussions. Yael had got us this meeting. Now, all we had to do was to impress the 15-odd GET members.

'See, everyone felt bad about the way the whole thing ended.' Yael told me over a cup of coffee sitting in her chic office in Camden, London. I had flown to London for a day to see her and understand what their plan with us was.

'Nobody got over ThreadSol at Coats and I think there is a good chance that we could pull this off now.' She then smiled and continued. 'And now I am back, so if we get going, we could end it swiftly.' She winked and added, 'It is a Ross and Rachel story. We seem to not be able to live apart or together!'

The conversation came at the right time. We were having a hard time getting investment for all the reasons I have already spoken about. The painful realization that India is not the place from where you can build a category-creating world-class product had started to dawn on me.

The Li & Fung experience told me that we needed far more money and time to execute the big million-dollar deals internationally with large apparel brands. And the fact that one of our existing investors had regulatory issues in investing in our Singapore parent company meant a very rough road for investments. We could still power through and get some investments, but then that would not be enough to expand into the Western Hemisphere where the brands' decision-making was.

So, we decided to work with Coats again. It was an effort to convince the board that this was the right thing to do. Thankfully, both Blume and Catamaran were supportive. I wondered if reigniting the fire with Coats would be suboptimal, but Yael had such strong conviction that we decided to give this a second go.

I woke up with a splitting headache the morning we were meant to present. I had excruciating body ache, a hoarse throat and a 103-degree fever. The one-hour car ride to the Sheraton Hotel was equally painful. I was curled up in the backseat with my head resting on Mausmi's lap. Every time the car stopped and accelerated in the traffic, I felt sick and nauseated. *How am I supposed to impress the bunch while I was barely able to stand upright?* I wondered. It looked like Mausmi would have to wing the meeting. It was not ideal, but then what could be done?

At 2 p.m., we were ushered into the grand boardroom of Saigon Sheraton. The room was occupied by 15 men, all in their late fifties or early sixties. All were wearing dark suits with mostly white shirts and dark ties. Half of them were balding. Almost everyone had glasses. All of them had black-coloured Windows laptops.

And in walked Mausmi and me. We were wearing blue faded denim with our bright grey and orange ThreadSol sweatshirts with our individual hashtags. We both had long hair and we carried thin stylish silver MacBooks. The difference could not be starker!

The moment I entered the room, I felt a huge rush of adrenaline – just like I would feel when I would walk up to my drum kit during a gig. Somehow all my pain and grogginess evaporated, and I was back at my showman's best. The 30-minute meeting stretched to 60 minutes. The presentation and the follow-on exchanges were brilliant. The GET laughed at our jokes, lauded our efforts and the conversation was free-flowing. Later, Hizmy said, 'You guys looked so refreshingly different and yet so professional; the GET was very impressed.'

As we came out of the meeting, I almost collapsed with exertion. The performance was over. It was time to deal with the fever again.

Istanbul, August 2018

Istanbul is the quintessential East-meets-West city, where the modern and ancient collide, producing a fascinating tapestry. It is a giant nerve centre of international trade. Here you can see the modern eighteen-wheeler giant trucks hauling freight from all parts of Europe to the retro-stylish trucks adorned with traditional Islamic motifs from Pakistan, Egypt, Iraq and Libya.

You will see Muslim dervishes with long white beards musing under a shady tree and a stone's throw away, you will spot a tattooed and pierced modern Turkish woman with dyed hair, drinking an arak.

The place is heaven for foodies. The delectable Adana kebabs, the mouthwatering Çiğ köfte, the scrumptious kokoreç, the dramatic-looking salt-crusted fish – Istanbul has food to die for. And there was Turkish çay (tea) and hookah everywhere.

Abhishek, Bratish, Mausmi and I were visiting Istanbul to meet with the Coats team to finalize the acquisition deal. Yael was there and so was Hizmy. We had two days of fantastic meetings with the Coats team. Yael ensured everything moved like clockwork. At the end of each day's meeting, with the satisfaction of having converged on so many important decisions, we all would go to some fantastic restaurant and gorge on Turkish food and the local arak with shalgam (a liquor that you drink with turnip juice).

Abhishek surprised us all by ordering a 'meter kebab', which was true to its name and just delicious. Abhishek delivered one of the finest gluttonous performances of all time and polished off the whole thing!

In 48 hours, all the key decisions were taken. Everything was the same as last time. We just had to ratify the same agreements that we had made last time. The deal price, the payout structure, the roles that the four founders will get inside Coats, the future of the ThreadSol team members, the next five years' business targets, the outlines for the various diligences that Coats would need to do with tentative timelines, the people who would be involved to get us across the line – all were discussed and agreed. It looked like there was serious urgency from Coats' side to get over the line this time.

With all meetings wrapped up, we went site-seeing. I had been to Istanbul half a dozen times before for ThreadSol's work but for my friends, this was their first trip. We spent a day marvelling at the city's architectural grandeur. Usually, in any city I came to for business, my head would always be full of work and I never absorbed the sights. With the acquisition's major issues sorted and in the fun company of my best friends, this Istanbul trip turned out to be the trip that I enjoyed the most.

As we landed in Delhi in the early hours of the next day, I saw an email from Rajiv, the CEO of Coats, who instructed all the Coats' generals to put the acquisition in high gear and complete this by end of December 2018. I think Rajiv's leadership was the key that made the processes move fast and full marks to Coats and their teams who did a great job toeing their CEO's line.

This time, we played smart. We did not commit our people to the diligence process. In fact, we hired a bunch of external consultants to work with us to help speed up the process. The legal, financial, technical, business and marketing diligence teams from Coats swooped down on us again. But, unlike the last time, this time Hizmy and Yael had a whip in their hands to make quick decisions on any issue that got stuck.

By mid-November, we looked well set to complete the diligence process. Everything was moving smoothly. Looked like there would be a happy ending to the Ross and Rachel story after all . . .

The infinity pool had a stunning view of the Indian Ocean. The sky was a clear light blue. I was half-submerged in the pool looking at the vast expanse of water. A chilled beer in my hand completed the state of bliss. I was in the tropical paradise of Sri Lanka. We had rented a glitzy super modern European-styled 30,000 square foot private villa, around 30 kilometres from Galle town – almost at the southern tip of Sri Lanka.

I had come with my close family. It was Mausmi and me, Wilson and his wife Rumi, Rashmi and her husband Arnab, and Jaya. Rumi and Rashmi were Mausmi's younger sisters. Jaya was Mausmi's cousin. Both Jaya and Wilson worked with us at ThreadSol. It was the last week of November 2018, and we had arrived in Sri Lanka for a few days of fun. The Coats' acquisition diligence was all in good shape and we looked forward to closing it by December.

'Looks like you are back to living your life, man. Sun, sand, private villa, pool, beers, friends . . . You got it all,' Bratish said to me on a video call. And then he said, 'This is how one imagines running your own business would look like.'

I smiled and took another gulp of my chilled beer. My life has been anything but chilling on tropical beaches with drinks that have little straw hats on them. I had been on the move for the last five years. Had not taken a single day off. Always fought with the present to build a future. Now that the acquisition was on the anvil, I could probably, for once, enjoy the proverbial tycoon moment of a relaxing tropical vacation. Yes, life is good. I sipped my beer. And right then I heard my phone give out a chime.

'Who could it be?' I picked up the phone and saw the email.

Hi Manasij,

The technical due diligence (DD) report has come negative. According to the report, it is not advisable to acquire ThreadSol as the technical depth of the products is not great. We are stopping all other diligence streams until this is cleared. See the attached technical DD report. Let me know your thoughts.

Yours,
Hizmy
CIO, Coats

My tropical vacation had been hit by a tsunami.

We had seen the technical DD report. It was a 140-page document made by a UK tech diligence consultancy that had visited our offices in Delhi and Kolkata a few weeks back. They had been hugely impressed by our processes and the depth of the products. The report had great feedback. How could a fantastic report create a negative sentiment?

A couple of frenetic calls later, I realized something has gone amiss inside Coats' systems. I could not understand it. But I realized I could not fix it sitting in a pool, drinking beer. I told Hizmy and Yael that I was dashing to London to get to the bottom of this. Thankfully they agreed. As I bought the flight tickets and got ready to leave for London, Mausmi gave me a stern warning.

'Manasij, we have 30 days of cash left. We need to get this deal. Do what you can. Get us this.'

We were watching the cash reserves closely but were not worried as we expected the deal to be done by mid-December. Now, if the DD gets stopped and the deal rolls forward to January 2019, we will be out of cash!

'What the hell just happened?' I was perplexed. 'What explains this, huh?' I said as I was jumping into the cab that would take me to the Colombo airport.

'It is a Ross and Rachel story. There is bound to be a last-minute drama,' Mausmi said wryly.

24

A Last-Minute Drama!

I landed in London at 6 a.m. on 30 November 2018. The uncomfortable economy class chair, a bunch of noisy fellow passengers and my anxiety over the acquisition meant that I had had an exhausting flight with very little sleep. That day, Heathrow's walkways looked endless. The queue in the main immigration hall was so long that it took me two hours to clear it.

In another hour, I checked into the el cheapo Ibis Hotel on Bath Road, five minutes from Heathrow Airport. The room was super small and the grey-and-white colour scheme was plain depressing. There were no windows in the room and a lone skylight was the only source of natural light. I had no idea that I was about to spend some excruciating days of my life in this pigeonhole of a room.

That afternoon, I went to see Yael in London. Yael looked as if she had aged 10 years since I met her. She was pensive and morose – a big departure from her usual upbeat self.

'Manasij, Coats is getting cold feet.' She sipped her coffee and told me sitting at her office desk. 'The thing is, not everyone inside Coats wants this deal. Many are saying that ThreadSol and Coats just cannot fit, that you guys are too different. They say, look at the CEO Manasij here – he has long hair and tattoos – how is this guy going to fit in with Coats? Then, every small issue that is thrown out by the diligence teams becomes another crisis of belief and provides ammunition for them to hang you guys.' Yael looked sad and broken.

'I have been fighting for you guys. I know with Coats' support, you guys can scale this business to terrific heights. We could become the technology partners to all the best apparel and fashion brands worldwide. I know you guys can make wonders happen with your AI platform. But that will happen when you come in. Right now, Coats is not in a happy place. I am not in a great place. My support for what is right for the business is taken as biased backing. So, I am taking a back seat,' she said with a grim chuckle.

'And this technical DD report has been the last nail in the coffin. Peter looks after Coats' internal technology division and he is in charge of looking at the technical DD report – and he has made a negative recommendation to Rajiv and Adrian. He has been negative about you guys from the beginning.' She stopped and looked outside the big glass windows. Rain was falling on the glass and the world outside looked distorted.

I was stunned. I had sensed that there was something amiss and that's why I flew to London, but I did not know the rot was this deep. I was thankful to Yael for her candour. It gave me the necessary clarity that was badly needed.

My next meeting with Hizmy was not as chatty as the one with Yael. However, Hizmy shared the 10-slide executive summary that Peter had prepared by reading the 140-page detailed technical diligence report. Hizmy was tight-lipped but I sensed that he did not believe Peter's deductions completely and therefore wanted me to look at it. It was this executive summary that had lit the match on the dry powder keg. I thanked Hizmy and went back to my pigeonhole hotel room. I sent the technical DD report and the executive summary to Abhishek and Bratish and asked them to do a review and find the issues.

And then I took a long hot shower. The tiring flight and the two back-to-meetings had left me almost dead. The long hot shower did a world's good to me. I went down to the hotel restaurant. They had only three main dishes to choose from. I chose an American hamburger and fries for dinner and as I waited for the food, I saw Bratish's WhatsApp message on the founders' group.

'This executive summary is complete bunkum. Sending you debunking pointers . . .'

The burger's patty was dry and tasteless, but I felt a glimmer of hope for the first time in the last 36 hours. We might be able to turn the tide.

~

The meeting was tense. The stakes were high. If we fail, the acquisition fails. I had to prove that Peter's deductions were wrong and yet not make it look like I was attacking him. I had to prove that our tech was sound, but I had to do this in a way that it doesn't create any enmity.

To make matters worse, it was an online meeting. Yael, Hizmy, Peter and some other Coats technology folks were in the meeting. On my special request, the UK-based consulting team that had done the tech DD was also invited to the call. Bratish, Abhishek, Mausmi and I were also there. I knew all of us were highly stressed.

After the regular pleasantries, Hizmy passed the meeting to me. I shared my screen and opened the 140-page detailed tech diligence report and the 10-page executive summary report side-by-side.

'Alright gentlemen and ladies, our objective is to learn from you guys about how can we do better in our technical efforts.' I began as diplomatically as possible.

'We should go through the executive summary observations and get everyone's opinions on how can we fix them.'

An hour later, we were completely vindicated. All the points in the executive summary report were found to be 'bunkum', just as Bratish had said. As it became clear that we were in the clear, Hizmy and Yael both became highly supportive. Sensing the change in the winds, Peter morphed his stance and alluded that he intended to merely initiate a constructive technical exchange to help us build even better stuff.

I thanked him profusely for giving us this opportunity to be a part of open dialogue and I mentioned that we solemnly looked forward to working with him. In my head, however, I wished I could dress up as a Japanese samurai, brandish my fearsome katana and plunge the cold metal blade into his chest and rip out his heart!

The next day, on the afternoon of 2 December , we got an email from Himzy.

> Hi Manasij,
>
> We are restarting all the diligence streams from today.
>
> Rajiv, the CEO of Coats, will meet you on Dec 4th evening in his office.
>
> If all goes well, on Dec 6th, the Coats Board meeting is where we can get the deal ratified.
>
> Yours,
> Hizmy
> CIO, Coats

Shortly after that, I received a WhatsApp from Yael.

'Congratulations. You guys handled the car wreck of a situation really well. There is a wrinkle that you need to handle. You may have won the technical diligence round, but it is not over.'

I looked at the message and wondered what the wrinkle could be. This was too much for a last-minute drama . . .

~

It was dark . . .

It was cold . . .

It was raining . . .

I was numb . . .

I was walking on the deserted road at 11 p.m. on a cold rainy December night. My head hurt. My heart ached. I was emotional and I was distraught.

I sat down at an empty bus stop and lit up a cigarette. The pieces of the evening came back flashing like a montage. It was as if I was seeing myself in an out-of-body experience . . .

There I am getting into the car that Coats had sent to take me to meet Rajiv, the CEO of Coats.

There I am waiting at the Coats office lounge.

There I am getting impatient and walking up and down the empty office aisles.

There I am glancing at my watch and wondering why my 7 p.m. meeting was getting delayed.

There I am making myself a cup of tea from the pantry at 8 p.m.

There I am getting some fresh air at 9 p.m.

And there I am entering Rajiv's room at 9.30 p.m.

I see Rajiv enter. We shake hands. We sit down. We sip tea. Rajiv is speaking. What is he saying? It's like I am hearing him talk in slow motion.

'My CFO says that deal will happen over his dead body.'

'But I want to do this.'

'But I have to agree with him too.'

'We will do the deal on one condition . . .'

And his phone rings.

He goes out of the room.

There I am sitting in Rajiv's office, wondering what that condition would be. Wondering why the CFO is so averse to this deal.

'Manasij, get us home. We need this deal.' I can hear Mausmi speaking.

There I see Rajiv entering the room again.

I see myself sitting in the chair, with my heart in my mouth – trying my best to act brave.

I again hear Rajiv speak. . .

'We will do the deal at $13 million.'

'You have two days to get your investors to agree.'

'If you agree, we go to the board on the sixth, else . . .'

Rajiv has spoken.

We are shaking hands . . .

There I am getting into the car to go back.

There I am getting out of the car.

There I am walking on the roads aimlessly in the cold and rain…

I felt lost.

I felt defeated.

I felt utterly hopeless.

A car came flying down the empty road and splashed cold, muddy water on me. I tasted mud in my mouth and snapped out of my thoughts.

I was back in my hotel room at midnight. I looked at my phone. The founders' WhatsApp group had no messages. Over the many years, my friends have learnt to never hassle me with details. They knew I was dealing with something important and that I would update them when I was able to gather myself. I loved them giving me so much space. It moved me today.

No, we did not deserve to be priced at $13 million. It was a low price – no questions – especially when we had agreed just a few months back on a higher number. We had built a fantastic product, a terrific team, a solid business and a watertight reputation in the market. This was worth more. But then, we had issues raising funds.

Coats had its own pressure points. The company had never acquired a start-up. This was a new unknown for them. Kudos to Rajiv, Adrian, Hizmy and Yael to have come this far. There must be naysayers saying things in their earshot. They are bound to respect those voices – however much they may seem unreasonable to me. The only thing that they seemed to agree with was de-risking their position by reducing the agreed deal price without bothering to give any explanation. Was it ethical? Who knows . . . it was surely not illegal! That is good enough for almost all the corporates when they take a decision.

I took a long warm shower and called my friends at 1 a.m., my time in London. It was 6.30 a.m. their time in India and they all came on the call. I walked them through the deal construct. I was surprised by how well my colleagues took the news.

'Let's just get moving Manasij. Let's just complete the deal.' Abhishek summed up for all of us. 'They know our finances as they are doing this detailed due diligence. They know you cannot go anywhere else so soon. They may have other pressure points, but why would a seasoned business miss such a good opportunity when they know that we cannot raise funds so quickly? Just complete the deal and come home, Manasij. No price tag determines the value of work. Let's just do this.'

Bratish and Mausmi agreed. They also told me I should get some shut-eye. I loved my friends and dearly wished they were with me. They gave me so much love and support that I felt good again.

As I got into bed, my head was still echoing Rajiv's words. 'We will do the deal at a $13 million price . . . We will do the deal at a $13 million price . . . We will do the deal at a $13 million price . . .'

Coats were having the board meeting in Central London on 6 December 2018. Hizmy was presenting the acquisition case and if the board supported it, we would get the deal. I was a stone's throw away from the board meeting venue, sitting in a really nice British pub named The Jugged Hare on Chiswell Street with my laptop. I could not sit idle in my depressing hotel room any more!

As I sipped my beer and waited for the news, I made a crucial decision. I decided that I would write a book about running ThreadSol. So, this book was actually conceived on Thursday, 6 December 2018, at The Jugged Hare pub, London, at around 1 p.m.

At 3 p.m., I got a text from Hizmy saying that the board had okayed the deal. Now, we had to complete the rest of the diligence work in 10 days. The last working day for Coats was 20 December. They wanted the deal to be done by then.

'Don't worry, Manasij. I will help you guys close all diligence points in the next 10 days.' Hizmy assured me over the phone. He had been super helpful over the last few days.

'Hope your investors are on board?' he asked.

'Yes, they are,' I told him.

Most of them had flipped out at this somersault from Coats. No one was happy. I was not happy either, but this was the only rational move left. Ashish from Blume had been super helpful in getting everyone to rally behind me. Finally, after many calls and many hours of negotiations, they all agreed. I had spent days sitting in a dark windowless room to convince the investors to take the deal. I was wiped out with this last-minute drama.

For the last one week, I lived with constant disappointment in my head. The anxiety and the insecurities took a heavy toll on me. I was relieved that it was over.

I landed in Delhi in the early hours of 8 December 2018.

'Where are you going?' The cab driver asked me.

As I sank in the cushioned rear seat, I muttered, 'Let's go home man, let's go home . . .'

25

Let's Go Home . . .

World War II ended in August 1945 with Japan's surrender. However, something astonishing happened after the war. All around Southeast Asia, many Japanese holdouts were found over the next three decades. These were all in isolated islands where the Japanese Imperial Army was cut off from communication and therefore didn't know the war was over and kept fighting.

The last confirmed holdout to be discovered was the remote Morotai Island in Indonesia in December 1974 – almost 30 years after the war was over! The heartbreaking fact was that no one in Japan worried about their soldiers having to fend for themselves. Their abandonment was a painful oversight from the rulers for whom they had fought loyally. What a shame!

When I walked into my office on Monday, 10 December 2018, I was suddenly reminded of these Japanese holdouts and their decades of neglect. I saw my people in the ThreadSol office going about their daily routines. These guys didn't know that in 10 days ThreadSol was going to be sold to Coats. I could not tell them either. Coats was clear about this. It was a public listed company, and any acquisition news moves the share prices. Therefore, secrecy was important.

And it all ended that night
A journey well done – it feels right!

Also, the deal price haircut would mean less money for the employees too. Coats wanted to pay the $13 million in tranches. The first tranche was to pay off the investors of ThreadSol. That would leave over a million dollars that we the founders could take in. Then the employees could get paid alongside us from the second tranche onwards. From the second tranche onwards, the money was dependent on the joint business plan. That was not a worry at all. We were very sure with Coats' backing, the numbers would be easily achievable.

However, when the four of us met, I found all of us were uncomfortable with this arrangement. We all wanted two things. First, we wanted our employees to be paid in the first tranche itself and second, we wanted them to get guaranteed payouts in the future – completely delinked to any targets, performance or any other encumbrances.

There are many stories of founders shortchanging their employees at the time of exit to enrich themselves. Every time we read such stories, we all squirmed in disgust. We certainly didn't want be remembered as and counted among such selfish founders. We wanted our employees to be rewarded now and we wanted it to be unconditional. If that meant that the four of us got zero money to start with – so be it!

Mausmi wrote an amazingly moving email to Coats that we wanted to pay our investors first and then our employees. We, as founders, wanted zero money from Coats in the first tranche. Needless to say, a staunch hardnosed business like Coats was surprised to receive this email.

'No one does this, Manasij. No one has seen anything like this in Coats where someone was willingly not dipping into money and choosing to enrich their employees instead,' Yael told me.

'You guys are made of strong moral timber.'

After a few rounds of back and forth, Coats agreed. Our employees would get all their money paid. They would be paid upfront from the first tranche and a small portion over the next few years without any conditions attached. Every employee would be retained, and their salaries would be revised using a market salary benchmarking for a $100 million revenue company as the standard yardstick. This meant, most of the employees could look forward to getting a handsome raise in their salaries and a good load of upfront cash. We had promised our employees stock plans and this was their payday too.

The founders would be paid in the later tranches as the business plan numbers came to fruition. Our strong pitch for our folks pushed our payouts into a further riskier zone. But we could not care less. That was the ethical thing to do. That was the right thing to do.

'I don't mind getting zero in the first tranche. I will sleep better when I go home knowing our people are getting their money,' Bratish said.

We all agreed. ThreadSol was nothing without the people. We could not thank our people enough. I don't know if greed is good or not. But I do know gratitude is. This was our way of showing gratitude to our people.

Once Coats confirmed this, for the first time we all felt happy. We all had smiles on our faces. My co-founders are people with exceptionally high moral courage. I have not seen them act petty for material things. They always made me a better person and this whole thing now felt just right to all of us. For the first time after the deal was struck, we celebrated.

I had done a podcast a few years back called *Outliers with Pankaj Misra*. In that, I had said that the founder must eat last. I had said that a founder must look out for their investors, employees and customers first – even if it means at the cost of their own self. I was happy to be able to walk the talk.

'I don't mind getting zero. I will sleep better when I go home.'

'Yeah Bratish, I agree with you mate. Let's go home . . .'

Meanwhile, the D-Day for the acquisition was decided. It would be on 19 December 2018. Rajiv, the CEO of Coats, and Adrian, the head of Coats Global Services – the tech division of Coats that was acquiring us – would fly to Delhi on that day. Our investors would fly in too. And on 19 December we would ink the deal. This was the tentative plan. Yael was not slated to travel to Delhi. Her omission was strange. It was her perseverance that had taken the ship this far.

The last mile plan depended on completing the due diligence (DD) in the next few days. The legal DD was again getting bogged down. As we saw last year, this was the major hurdle. This part was again getting into tangles. We knew if we took our eyes off this, it could collapse again. So, we were on top of everything like hawks.

All four of us would start the day at 6 a.m. to begin working with the lawyers in Singapore, Indonesia and Vietnam. Then, as the day progressed, we would have meetings with the legal experts in India, followed by meetings with the legal teams in the UK. We would finish the day around 2 a.m. and then restart at 6 the next day. There were daily progress checks with Coats and though the deadline was stiff, we were making decent progress.

On the other side, we decided to issue an RTB (Return to Base) call to all our folks in Bangladesh, Vietnam, Indonesia, China, Sri Lanka, etc. Every year, the ThreadSol team congregated one time in December, and we thought we could club our annual festivities and the acquisition together to make it a proper celebration time for the team.

So, ThreadSol geared up for an annual festivity. The band was preparing a few rock covers. The dance troupe was preparing a few foot-tapping numbers. The literary society was preparing a few skits, poetry and stand-ups. We also decided to book a few buses to go to Agra the day after the deal was signed and booked a whole discotheque for the team to wash the evening down with drinks and dance. Everything was moving smoothly.

As fate would have it, on 18 December, one day before the deal inking, we got stuck in one serious hurdle. One of the Coats' overzealous lawyers flagged some potential taxation issues that could happen in the future and wanted us to indemnify Coats. In plain language, it meant if, at a future date, the government wants Coats to pay taxes on a certain item (the chances of that happening are supremely remote), then the ThreadSol founders and investors would have to pay that tax. This was a major surprise item for all of us.

Meanwhile, Rajiv and Adrian had taken the flight out of Heathrow and were supposed to land in Delhi at 10 a.m. They were supposed to come to our office in Noida at 1 p.m. and were supposed to interact with our investors and our team members.

'Manasij, if by 6 p.m. IST tomorrow, we do not resolve this pickle, the acquisition would go on hold. In that case, Rajiv and Adrian's visit would just be a courtesy visit,' Hizmy sounded an ominous warning to me.

I was drumming with the band for a quick one-hour practice for the gig tomorrow when Hizmy called and gave me this information. I was deeply troubled. Here we are, the whole of ThreadSol, planning for festivities for tomorrow, everyone has travelled from far and wide to be here for the big event tomorrow and worse of all, we are running low on cash, and we need this deal to go through.

If we don't, then ThreadSol will crash and burn! And everyone will say when ThreadSol was burning, Manasij was playing the drums – just like the infamous Roman emperor Nero was when Rome was burning!

We resumed the practice after the call but I fumbled so many times that my band members got cross.

'What is wrong with you, dude?' Shivam, our lead guitar and the band's undisputed boss, admonished me. 'Why are you so distracted?'

I wish I could tell him. I took a deep breath instead.

'Nothing. Sorry guys. Let's take it from the top,' I apologized and picked up the sticks again.

The whole night of 18 December was spent on stressful calls with the UK legal teams with no resolution. We worked with the Coats' lawyers, our lawyers, our investors' lawyers till 5 in the morning to sort this out, and yet it remained a logjam. It looked as if the story was leading to a rough landing the next day.

The D-Day of 19 December 2018 dawned. At 6 a.m., we were back at the office. The calls with the Singapore lawyers started again. We had had a night with zero sleep and the complicated legal issues early in the morning were a painful start. Strong black coffee and a few cigarettes kept me going and we powered through to get to some common ground.

At 1 p.m., the Coats jamboree landed in our office. Rajiv and Adrian camped in the boardroom with Ashish from Blume and Rounak from Catamaran representing our investors. The Coats India head and the Coats HR head of India were also present.

Abhishek and I were tasked to be with the Coats delegation and officiate the meetings with the investors and then follow it up with a meeting with the key team members of ThreadSol.

Mausmi and Bratish were still in frenetic calls to sort out the kinks. It was a stressful meeting. While I had concentrated on keeping Rajiv and Adrian entertained as they dissected our product, process, people, the joint business plan post-acquisition, etc. I kept my one eye on the WhatsApp group of the founders where Bratish and Mausmi were posting regular updates. So far, there was nothing to cheer me up.

It was 5 p.m. It was time to usher the key team members to meet the Coats delegation. I got a breather and went straight to the first-floor meeting room where Bratish and Mausmi were holding the fort.

Mausmi had worked out a solution with an external consultant – or so she thought.

'You need to relay this to Hizmy and see if he agrees. If he agrees to this solution, then you need to call the lawyers from our side and get them to agree. If they all agree by 6 p.m., we have the deal.' Mausmi was calm and clear.

I took the notes from Mausmi and headed to the next meeting room. I had a quick call with Hizmy and he promised to come back to me in the next 30 minutes. I immediately called our lawyers and told them about the possible resolution. They also agreed to come back in 30 minutes.

In 30 minutes, we would know our fate! I went downstairs and lit a cigarette and sipped my black coffee. Five years of effort and toil was culminating in this 30-minute wait! I was tense.

'They are about to finish in the next 30 minutes,' I saw Abhishek's message in the group.

'Stall. We need more time,' I replied.

'I will try . . .' Abhishek replied.

My phone rang. It was Hizmy.

'Manasij, this is agreeable. We can do this. Have your lawyers agreed?' he asked.

'Let me check and call you right back,' I said.

'I can stall at best 10 more minutes, Manasij,' Abhishek's message was almost beseeching for a reprieve. He was finding it hard to extend the meeting.

I called my lawyers.

'Hey guys, Coats had agreed to our solution. Are we good to go?' I asked.

'Manasij, we should think about this more. We think given the scenario . . .'

I had had enough of this legal mumbo-jumbo. This was now or never. It was 6 p.m. and we had run out of time. If we couldn't get this across the line, we were dead!

So, I cut him short and said, 'Look, guys, this is it. I need a yes or no. If this is a no, there is no deal. And I want this deal. So, what do you say, yes or no?'

The folks on the other side fell silent. They didn't like my insistence.

'Yes, we are good.'

'Thanks, guys. Appreciate it,' I hung up.

I called Hizmy, 'Hey, Hizmy, we are good to go.'

'Okay, Manasij. I will send you the final draft agreement with the amendments.' He then paused and said, 'Congratulations, you got yourself a deal!'

As the call ended. I sat down on the main entrance stairs and cupped my face with my palms. The intense pressure and tension of the last 36 hours were finding a release. And then I suddenly realized that my friends don't know that it was done. I needed to relieve them from their agonies too.

I opened my WhatsApp and typed.

'Coats agreed. We have a deal. It is over. Let's go home!'

Everyone read the message. I knew all of us were just experiencing nothing but an unbounded true sense of relief. Finally, Mausmi replied, 'We had six days of cash left.'

Wow!

The rest of the evening was a flurry of activities. The deal was signed at 6.30 p.m. All the members of ThreadSol congregated in our third-floor hall. The stage was set. It was time to officially announce the acquisition. I was supposed to make the announcement. After that Rajiv would speak and the festivities would kick off with performances from the band, dance troupe, stand-ups, etc.

As I took to the podium, a strange feeling crept inside me. This would be the last time I would address my people as the CEO of the business. All these years I had done many all-hands meetings where I had addressed my colleagues and I had always been crystal clear as to what I wanted to convey. Today, I was blank. The emotional drain of the last few weeks had wrecked me from within and my soul was bankrupt of any energy. This was the speech where I was to hand over the baton to Coats and it seemed way harder than I had imagined. ThreadSol was our baby. I was to give it away . . .

All these years I had represented ThreadSol on so many platforms, in many competitions, in many symposiums, on many stages in many events, in many television interviews and even in a TEDx talk, and today I felt tongue-tied. Maybe this is how a father feels giving his beloved daughter away. It is probably bittersweet. And that is probably why the bride's father is never asked to make a speech. It must be hard seeing a piece of your heart detach. The emotional maelstrom of this separation must be hard.

As I stood on the podium, I was overwhelmed. I somehow managed to convey the acquisition story. A raucous, thunderous applause swept over the hall. A hundred and thirty ThreadSol folks clapped and cheered as on my cue, Wilson and Nikita peeled the sticker from a giant whiteboard exposing the text – 'ThreadSol is now Coats'. The folks had an inkling that something momentous was about to happen and they welcomed it with their typical enthusiastic gusto. As the hall went berserk, I watched Abhishek, Bratish and Mausmi. They were looking at our people. They had smiles on their faces.

'I hope Coats will take care of you guys as good, if not better, as we have tried to do as founders. From here onwards, it is their baby. The next stage of the script will be written by them.'

I paused for a moment and uttered the last sentence as the co-founder and CEO of ThreadSol.

'And with that, ladies and gentlemen, I would like to welcome on stage, the CEO of Coats . . . your CEO . . . my CEO – Rajiv Sharma!'

As Rajiv made his way to the stage, I went to the end of the hall and picked up a beer and sat on the last row. I was done! All I wanted now was to sit and sip my beer in peace.

The evening rolled into a super fun one. All the performances were terrific. The dinner was great. There were a lot of handshakes and hugs. Finally, the Coats delegation left and so did the investors. We were alone with our people.

All the old-timers sat down around the main entrance stairs with beers in their hands. We sipped the cold beer and told stories of the bygone days. No new stories – just the old evergreen hits that we had told many a time, heard many a time – but these stories were important as they had knitted the clan together for so many years. We laughed and laughed and laughed. Some of the folks cried. Yes, it was an emotional day.

I felt relaxed and relieved. The time with my friends on the stairs healed me. I shed all the stress, the tension, the anxieties . . . As our old deckhands cracked one joke after another, my negativities melted away and I was happy again.

Around 1 a.m., we decided to call it a night. The next morning, all the folks of ThreadSol were going to the Taj Mahal one last time as a group and we planned to leave at 6. As people started to pack up and leave, the four of us hung around saying our goodbyes to everyone.

Finally, it was just the four of us left.

We stood silently at the entrance of our office at the root of the flight of five steps that took you to the main lobby. The five steps were covered at the top by a projected ledge acting as a roof. And on that roof was the big neon lettering 'ThreadSol' in our orange and black corporate colours. We sat there silently. There was nothing to talk about really. We were just soaking in the incredible journey and the momentous day.

How improbable this all was! When we began the journey, we had no money, no connections in the VC world, no connections in the customer spaces, no experienced team members and no idea of how to run a business, let alone an international business. At every step of the journey, there were hitherto unseen encumbrances that looked insurmountable. There were many soul-crushing rejections.

Three times we almost touched bankruptcy and risked dying. And yet, somehow, we survived. Not just survived – thrived actually. And in the process, we became the first apparel tech start-up in the whole world to scale our business and sell it too! That is some feat! Sure, the acquisition price could have been higher – but the satisfaction of building, scaling and getting acquired against all odds was the prize that seemed to compensate for all the minor glitches.

I have been asked many a time that I must feel very proud for having completed the full circle of build-raise-scale-sell for a start-up. I always reply that I do not feel proud. I feel very satisfied. I feel privileged that so many young dynamic passionate souls believed us to join the cause that the four of us founders embodied. In the end, we had a 30-people core team that rallied around us with rock-solid conviction and determination – every bit as good as the founders. We always thought of them as an extended co-founding team.

This story would not have happened without them. I have done tremendous injustice in not naming and applauding all of them in this book, but then they scripted this with their blood, sweat and tears and maybe they will forgive me for not naming them. This story also would not be possible without the countless folks who supported us and believed in us by becoming customers, investors or just plain well-wishers.

The mega successes of start-ups are fuelled by forces beyond the control of the founders. A devastating pandemic has been a boon for education tech, health tech, online meeting tech, e-commerce, etc. It has spelt doom for travel tech, ride-sharing tech, etc. When the winners and losers will count their chips, can anyone say with their hand on their heart that they could predict a pandemic? Can they deny the hand that sheer dumb luck played?

Just like the pandemic, many things are not in the control of the founders. As you embark on a journey you always prioritize certain things over others and make certain bets. You hope that you got the priorities right and you would not encounter a storm that would rip your ship apart that exposes the bets taken. If that happens, the only choice you have is to move on as you could have never foretold the storm while ashore. You need steely execution, dedicated conviction, a committed team, unwavering belief, unshaken faith from investors and happy and vociferously supporting customers to succeed, but to make it to the Ivy League, you need an invisible helping hand of timing and a stroke of luck or both.

When we began ThreadSol, we were the only apparel tech start-up in India. Five years later, when we sold to Coats, we were still the only apparel tech start-up in India. We had a huge lead over the market. We were a category creator in the true sense. But then, in India, category creators are not treated kindly. India still looks at the US and China for that. Hopefully, that will change with time. How would ThreadSol's story be if we were met by a visionary investor? Who knows? But, as I said, I feel satisfied that we completed an arduous journey and had the tenacity and energy to see it through, thereby becoming the first apparel tech start-up to make an exit!

How would I have reacted if, on the day we had decided to plunge into the start-up ocean, someone had asked me whether I would like to end up with 150 super-large customers, raking in over $12 million from customers in four years, expand our business to 16 countries, grow it 170 per cent per year on an average and finally sell it for an all-cash deal of ₹100 crore ($13 million)? Would I have taken it on day one? I think I would have taken it any day!

Yes, ₹100 crore exit is not big. Big exits are $100 million–$1 billion plus ones. That gives the bragging rights. That makes you a poster boy of the start-up stories that we all read. That makes you a business class or a first class founder as opposed to my economy class stature. My seed round investors made 20x return on their money. The Series A investors didn't make a fistful lot as the valuation dropped in the last minute – but they didn't lose any capital either. A game where 90 per cent of VC bets return a dead rat, this was not a terrible result but neither was it something one could brag about at a party. I think of ThreadSol as a modest success. I always said that the big billion-dollar start-up stories one gets to hear are start-up porns. That doesn't happen in real life for almost all. Those are exceptional outliers.

Yet, we love and adore them. Ask yourself, why do we do that? Is it because they made great innovations? Or simply because we just tend to respect people with more money and assume people with more money ought to be somehow more talented? I am surely not celebrated. I am okay with that. The economy class seat is still not bad. At least I am on the plane where 99 per cent just don't make it. Many of them who did not make it are probably more innovative and more deserving than me. This book is a hurrah for them.

Personally, this journey was enriching for me. I would like to believe that I came out a better person in the end. I am much more patient. I appreciate people more. I value people more. I care for people more. I don't get disheartened by rejections easily. I value cooperation over competition more. I understand that building anything is an endeavour imbued with persistent effort, clarity of communication and diligence in execution. And I understand and appreciate that most things are beyond my control and therefore all one can do is put the best foot forward and hope it works out.

Innovation will continue to happen around us. For example, I believe some spectacular innovations are in the offing. The biggest personal medicine and healthcare start-up is yet to be born. There will be a business that will allow you to get personalized medicine and organs based on your genetic makeup. That will become the world's most valuable business – possibly valued in trillions of dollars. But I can assure you that the first few attempts at that would not produce the trillion-dollar outcomes.

The first in the cavalry takes in more fire than the others and they eventually do not make it. But the relentless push from the rear flanks sees the beachfront won finally. Almost all the first movers have not made it super-duper big. I look at ThreadSol like that. Before us, no apparel tech start-up made anything worthwhile on the world stage. We did that. It was hard and at times bestial.

And there we were . . . four of us were sitting on the stairs of our office, having completed the arduous feat. We chit-chatted for a while. Abhishek and I shared a smoke. Bratish made some funny comments. Mausmi smiled all the way through. It was a peaceful night.

Finally, Abhishek got up. He walked to the lobby switchboard that controlled the neon lights over the stairs. He flipped the switch and instantly the orange-black neon light lettering of ThreadSol that was never ever shut down for a minute in the last five years fell into ghostly darkness. That was it. It was over!

As we all watched the extinguished ThreadSol lettering, Mausmi said, 'Let's go home.'

Epilogue: The Next Book in the Making

Munich, February 2020

It was mid-February 2020, right before the world drove off the cliff with COVID-19 and all travel ceased. I was flying back to Delhi from a meeting with Microsoft in Atlanta.

A year ago, I had sold my start-up to Coats. My bank account had more digits than I had ever seen in my life. As a part of the deal, I was now a high-ranking honcho on the corporate ladder with great perks and a fabulous eight-figure salary.

Gone were the days when I slogged out in the economy class, fighting for legroom on red-eye flights while my co-passenger snored on me. With my newfound stature, I was now entitled to business class flights with chilled drinks, flatbeds and smiling aircrew at my service.

A year ago, when the start-up hustle was at its ferocious prime, I would scramble a last-minute weekend getaway with Mausmi to a nearby hill station from Delhi in a half-decent resort with awful food and would still feel guilty about missing work over the weekend. Now, we took a leisurely three weeks off in New Zealand with great wine, juicy lamb chops and a top-of-the-line Mustang GT Convertible as our chariot. There were long leisure vacations with friends to Turkey, Spain, UK . . .

I was really enjoying my cushiony lifestyle. That day in February, on my return leg to Delhi, I had a stopover in Munich. The ground crew in Munich informed me that I was being upgraded to first class. Wow! I was ecstatic.

Just before the boarding, I went to a coffee shop and ordered a latte. The shop was crowded, so I had to sit at a table that was occupied. That's when I met this guy. He was sipping his coffee and looking pale and tired. We got talking and he told me that he was a founder of a fledgling start-up. When we started discussing his product, his tiredness just disappeared and his eyes glowed and his voice became animated. He was excited. His infectious zeal moved me. I was impressed.

Shortly after that, we took off. The first class is amazing. It is like having your own mansion 30,000 feet in the air. The pampering with chilled champagne and a procession of courses was incessant. I felt like a king. After a lovely meal of lobsters and brandy, I stepped out of my luxury cocoon and peeked into the cattle-class economy cabin. It was night-time. The lights were dimmed. A few entertainment screens were on and I saw the founder peering into his laptop and whipping up a storm on his keyboard.

That guy used to be me, I thought. Not long back, on all overnight flights, I would review designs, draft replies to emails, straighten out my presentations, do my expense logging . . . And nowadays I was shrouded in luxury and comfort and watched movies. I racked my brains. What did I remember about my meetings in Atlanta? The after-meeting dinner spread of brisket and the wine were great but the meeting was bland and nothing had stimulated my thoughts.

That's when I had my epiphany. I didn't want this – no more. I needed to be in the economy seat – tired to the bone, scared shitless but never short of inspiration and drive.

30,000 feet in the air, ensconced by the opulence of the first class, I realized that I belonged to the back of the plane where you fight for the legroom, you fight for another inch to recline your seat, you fight fatigue and demons in your head but you are always inspired and always raring to go.

I knew I was quitting; I knew I was starting up again . . .

Mumbai, March 2023

I was at Blume VC's office. By now, Blume had grown from a humdrum team of 10-odd folks in 2013 to a 100+ strong team and is largely regarded as the ace seed round investor in the Indian start-up circuit. The thing that struck me was the wall of fame at their office. It contained the names of all Blume start-ups that exited and made money. ThreadSol was there. I stopped and rubbed my thumb over the embossed lettering of the nine-inch plate. That's the end of years of toil – a nine-inch plate with your name!

Blume led the seed round of my current start-up – ZapScale. We raised $2.5 million in the seed round, valuing ZapScale at $8.5 million (₹70 Cr). It is funny to think that last time my seed round was just ₹1 crore at a valuation of ₹5 crore. For that, I had had to plead with 119 investors for over two years. With the success of ThreadSol, the round raise for ZapScale took just over a few months and we started at a 70 per cent valuation of my last exit!

I have learnt some important lessons from the last stint.

First, for ZapScale, we did super deep diligence of the market size, potential customers, their paying capacity, etc. before we began. This had been missing in my last journey. Last time, we just fell in love with the problem, and the business building was an afterthought and more of an on-the-job learning. This time, it is the other way around. I like to joke and say that your first start-up you do for love – the second one you do for the money.

Second, I learnt that I need to be in the fundraising mode forever. I devote a significant portion of my time making connections and talking to VCs even though I do not need money immediately. These are long-term cultivations and therefore one must be patient in building these relationships and growing them over time is the way to get the fruits of the labour.

Third, I learnt that I need to be prepared to lose friends. Start-ups are tough. Not everyone will have the energy to fall down again, gather themselves and run. In ThreadSol, I lost a few friends who did not speak to me again. The separation was professional, but it scars you personally. However, that is no reason to put up with underperformance and a lack of dedication and focus. A start-up aims to condense 10 years of work into two. The intensity will always be high and if someone cannot match it, better let them go. The abandoned souls can blame me – but deep down they know that they could not sustain the intensity. I have made peace with this.

Fourth, I know that raising money or selling the business takes time and one must aim to reach these milestones with at least six months or more money in the bank. We risked dying way too many times last time. The fear of death is not the best thought in your head. You do not want that. So, raise more. Keep more buffers and act early with sufficient gas in the tank. That gets you better deals and better outcomes.

Fifth, in ThreadSol, I kept everything on the backburner other than my start-up priorities. In a way, I missed out on life and life events. I missed Bratish's wedding, his daughter's birth and his open-heart surgery. I was not there with him during these important events. I was busy running ThreadSol. This time, I am making amends. I spend more time with my friends and family. I have a dozen-odd folks in my life who are 'my people' and I make it a point of spending time, making memories, doing fun trips with them throughout the year.

Sixth, I have gone back to my hobbies. My books, my sports, my fitness, my running, my passion for writing, my drumming, my hiking, my cycling, my love for music, movies and theatre – all have made a welcome comeback in my life. I have compartmentalized my start-up time and insulated it from impinging on things that I always loved to do.

Seventh, and last, I worry less and enjoy the ride more. Start-ups are chaotic and there is skill and chance both involved to become super successful. We can only control the skill part and the chance part is out of anyone's reach. A start-up is more like a game of poker. You know all about the hand odds, pot building, calling and betting – all necessary skills – but you cannot control what cards will be dealt – that's chance. I accept that a lot is not in my control and do not worry about it too much.

There are other learnings on executing better, doing better in delegating, doing better in defining work items and their success criterion, etc. However, the seven learnings above are the major takeaways for me.

Now, in my second stint, the world seems to value me more – akin to a newcomer in Bollywood who has just delivered one silver-screen hit and therefore is getting bigger banner projects. Perhaps, the rich think I am good to bet on. People, in any case, treat me like I am much richer than I am actually – I laugh at that in my head.

I do not know if ZapScale will be a super success and worth another book. This time I am foraying into building a software that will be sold in the US and EU. My customers will be super-savvy technology firms and smart-tech start-ups. These are a world apart from ThreadSol's clients,who were largely non-tech-savvy manufacturers of apparel from Asia.

Many have expressed surprise at this polar opposite choice. Wouldn't I be better off building for the apparel industry where we already know the ropes and have tons of connections and goodwill? I chuckle. Where is the fun in that?

'You could have been richer if you did a stint in known waters, Manasij.' I have heard many saying this to me.

They miss the point. I choose to build a start-up because I believe I am equal parts creative, analytical and methodical. Every stint that I do must appeal to all these fraternities. Going back to the same industry will bode well for the analytical and methodical part, but the creative axis will disappear.

I do not dream of being super rich. I dream of having the most stories, a life full of drama and adventures, a life full of surprises and inspiration. More zeroes in the bank account do not match up to these. Perhaps I am stupid. Perhaps this is why I am forever destined to remain the economy class founder.

Acknowledgements

There would be no *Economy Class Founder* without the tireless efforts of hundreds of folks at ThreadSol. Some are named in the book but a majority are not. Please know you are the ink and paper behind the words – you may be unnamed but are certainly not unappreciated.

Anjana and Suhas, my parents, who introduced me to loving books and encouraged me to write. My writings in magazines, newspapers, blogs and, eventually, this book, can all be traced back to their endeavours. I have been guilty of not thanking them enough. So setting the record straight here.

Mausmi, Jaya, Rashmi, Arnab, Wilson, Rumi, Nikita, Kundan, Bratish, Paulami, Sushmita, Devyane, Mitali – you guys are my people and my strength, and without your support this could have never happened. Alan (Yash), thank you for your illustrations. I wish you would become an artist soon.

Finally, Chiki and team Juggernaut – I sent you something akin to a child drawing a coloured circle, and you guys did your wizardry to turn that into this book! Many thanks.

A Note on the Author

Manasij is a serial entrepreneur and is currently building his second start-up, ZapScale. He is also an avid book reader, a drummer for his rock band, a mountain biker, runner, blogger, TEDx speaker, movie-music and theatre lover and a hobbyist murder-mystery writer. He is a sports superfan and follows cricket, football, tennis, F1, World Rally Championship, cycling and chess. He loves math, tech and engineering and is crazy about cars, trains and planes. And now, he is an author!